Read America(s):
An Anthology

Edited by

Hari Alluri, Garrett Bryant
& Amanda Fuller

LOCKED HORN PRESS | *San Diego, CA*

Poetry is a matter of life, not just a matter of language.

—Lucille Clifton

Read America(s): An Anthology
©2016

published by Locked Horn Press

www.lockedhornpress.org

Selection, notes, and introduction copyright © 2016 Hari Alluri, Garrett Bryant, Amanda Fuller, and Locked Horn Press. All rights reserved. No part of this book may be reproduced, stored in a retrieval system, or transmitted in any form, or by any means, electronic or manual, without prior written permission from Locked Horn Press or, where applicable, the content's copyright holders. Copyright of each poem remains with its author and other rights holders as cited in the Credits on pages 197-201, which constitute an extension of this copyright statement.

Printed in the United States of America

Cover Design:	Garrett Bryant
Book Design:	Garrett Bryant
Logo Design:	Cassie Byers
Cover Photo:	Étienne-Jules Marey

ISBN: 978-0-9903599-2-0

BOOK EDITORS
Hari Alluri
Garrett Bryant
Amanda Fuller

CONTRIBUTING BOOK EDITORS
Carolann Caviglia Madden
Carly Joy Miller

ART DIRECTOR
Garrett Bryant

LHP ADVISORY BOARD
Sandra Alcosser
Marilyn Chin
Kate Gale
Erik Haensel
Ashaki M. Jackson
Ilya Kaminsky
Cynthia Dewi Oka

CONTENTS

INTRODUCTION	Dear Reader,	13

•

Elmaz Abinader	Heartwood	20
	Needlework	22
Elizabeth Acevedo	La Santa Maria	24
	La Ciguapa	25
James E. Allman, Jr.	Orientation	27
Kofi Awoonor	America	29
Sherwin Bitsui	*from* Dissolve	30
	from Dissolve	31
Mario Bojórquez *Translated by Hari Alluri, Binh H. Nguyen and Jonathan Rodley*	A orillas del río Delaware frente a Camden y mirando las luces del Walt Whitman Bridge	32
	At the banks of the Delaware River Waterfront facing Camden and watching the lights of the Walt Whitman Bridge	33
	Museo Guggenheim	34
	Guggenheim Museum	35
Daniel Borzutzky	Dream Song #16	36
Geoff Bouvier	Invitation Only	37
	The Paradox of the Heap of Troubles	38
Derrick Weston Brown	Despite	40
	Halle Tells How They Broke Him	41
Jericho Brown	On Daniel Minter's High John the Conqueror	45
	Layover	46

Alí Calderón	*from* Constantinopla	47
Translated by Ana Bosch and	*from* Constantinopla	48
Karla Cordero	[Kentucky]	49
	[Kentucky]	50
Grady Chambers	Lake Shore Limited, Hour Seventeen	51
	Dispatch: Bamyan, Helmand, Baghlan, Ghor, 2008	52
Nadia Chaney	Physical Education Grade Six	54
	Wintering Place	55
Jennifer Chang	This Corner of the Western World	58
Briceida Cuevas Cob	U áak' abil tuchibil uj	59
Translated by Carolann Caviglia	Night of the Eclipse	60
Madden	In k'aaba'	61
	My Name	62
Karla Cordero	This Skin Be	63
	El Rancho '92	64
Cynthia Cruz	Sparks, Nevada	65
	Twelve in Yellow-Weed at the Edge	66
Kyle Dargan	Looking East as a Man Repairs Lights on the South Street Pier	67
	China Cycle XI: "Beautiful Country	68
Meg Day	*Teenage Lesbian Couple Found in Texas Park with Gunshot Wounds to the Head*	70
Sunshine Dempsey	Tiresias in Love	71
Natalie Diaz	Other Small Thundering	74
	A Woman with No Legs	76
Camille Dungy	'Tis of thee, sweet land (a poem of found text)	77
	There Are Seven Things I Know, And None of Them Is You	78

Jesus Antonio Esparza	A Hum Falling from Mi Abuela's Mouth	79
Jill Alexander Essbaum	I Am Most Myself	80
Tarfia Faizullah	100 Bells	81
Katie Farris	What We See in the Dark	82
M.K. Foster	Because You Said *I Told You We Have Rock Rivers, But No Water*	84
Clifton Gachagua	Cars	85
Carmen Giménez Smith	Radicalization	86
	from Post Identity	87
Graça Graúna *Translated by Carolann Caviglia Madden*	Manifesto - I	88
	Manifesto 1	89
	Caos climático	90
	Climate Chaos	91
francine j. harris	sift	92
Bob Hicok	Speaking American	94
Lizz Huerta	milking	96
Ishion Hutchinson	A Surveyor's Journal	98
Lauren Jensen-Deegan	Only You, My Husband as Smokey the Bear	99
	The Slow Race	100
Amaud Jamaul Johnson	Pigmeat	102
Claire Kageyama-Ramakrishnan	Terzanelle: Manzanar Riot	103
Ilya Kaminsky	We Lived Happily During the War	104
Joan Naviyuk Kane	the claim of the cliff above me (or, ancient and brutal)	105
	an other lethe	106

Katherine Larson	Love at Thirty-Two Degrees	107
Mariama J. Lockington	prunus persica	110
Tariq Luthun	New Rule	111
Thomas Lux	Lump of Sugar on an Anthill	112
Travis Macdonald	Oklahoma	113
	Maine	114
David Maduli	St. Mary's Park Ghazal	115
Nick Makoha	Prayers for Exiled Poets	116
Sally Wen Mao	Provenance: A Vivisection	117
Adrian Matejka	Map to the Stars	122
	EMPD Feat. Emily Dickinson	123
	Sounds of Earth	124
Erika Meitner	By Other Means	126
Jennifer Minniti-Shippey	Last Days of June	127
Michael Mlekoday	The History of the Black Market	128
	The History of the Lumberjack	130
Felix Mnthali	Neocolonialism	132
Carrie Moniz	Year Two of Your Seven-Year Sentence: Midnight Ride to Yuma	133
David Mura	Summers with the JACL	134
Angel Nafis	Gravity	135
Diana Khoi Nguyen	Self-Portrait with Strider Wolf	136
	from Matrilineal: Life *Au Naturel*	138
Nicole Parizeau	Bridgework	139
Patrick Rosal	Delenda Undone	144

Craig Santos Perez	America's Third Coming	146
	The American	147
Staci R. Schoenfeld	The Deconstruction of Dorothy Parker	148
Matthew Shenoda	from *Tahrir Suite*, III: The Migration	149
Javier Sicilia	Lo abierto	154
Translated by David Shook	What Is Open	156
Richard Siken	Detail of the Fire	158
	Landscape with a Blur of Conquerors	159
Jane Springer	Salt Hill	161
Brian Teare	Genius Loci	162
Truth Thomas	The Bloody Red Wheelbarrow	168
	Urban Warming	169
Brian Turner	Sadiq	171
	Phantom Noise	172
Sarah Vap	bluebells. blueballs. ballerinas.	173
Annie Won	Untitled	174
	Untitled	176
Monika Zobel	The Immigrant Searches the Map for Countries Larger Than His Palm	178

•

CONTRIBUTOR BIOGRAPHIES   181

•

CREDITS   197

INTRODUCTION

Dear Reader,

Last night, one of our editors was in conversation with two dear friends and they agreed that how we see the stars is how we see the world. They were speaking about different renderings of the stars into constellations, specifically Navajo, Roman, Mayan, Chinese and Kumeyaay (and Kumeyaay territory is where most of the LHP editors write and read). They noticed how many of the traditions called upon some of the same stars and, of course, how constellations tend to reflect the worldviews of the cultures that learned to see them. It may sound almost cute in the current socio-political climate to think of the sky as somehow inherently multicultural, but to do so can remind us how language is an evolving cultural perception and an ever-changing reflection. So too with any major idea—"America," for instance, which, for us, is a question that calls for a multi-contextual response.

Rather than offering poetry from just the United States of America or poetry from North, South and Central America, *Read America(s)* offers poetry from various renderings of "America" as more than simply a physical location occupying the Western Hemisphere. You will read poems by poets not located in any particular "America" who tell vital, often urgent, truths to America(s). You will find myriad cartographies and imaginings of America(s). You will also likely find, as we do, a feeling of incompletion: many more poems could be a part of this anthology and still that feeling of incompletion should persist. What is rendered here is one collection, a collection we hope points to the existence of and necessity for further responses.

It must also be acknowledged that poetry on the land known as "America" is thousands of years old, and that the nation-state is a relatively young idea. Its rise not only corresponds with the concept of race, European colonialism and the trans-Atlantic slave trade, but also has implications for the imagining, codifying and policing of gender and sexuality. Speaking of policing, these risings shape many contemporary forms of violence that give rise to responses in this text. And, while a volume of this size cannot pretend to completely honor a pre-"America" space and time, we include poems written in pre-colonial languages. Briceida Cuevas Cob has poems herein that appear in their indigenous language as well as their English translations, and Graça Graúna, while writing in Portuguese, is dedicated to indigenous causes in Brazil. Although the process of translation refracts with a foreign lens, and in these cases, through a double lens with Spanish as intermediary, to experience these poems in two languages simultaneously is to witness their reverberation in time. This echo serves, in part, to challenge us to see, hear and feel beyond the lens of modernity, to experience a more complete story outside of our own perception.

One of the most beautiful experiences that came with imagining and co-editing this project was reading poems to each other out loud and watching each other's facial expressions when a particular piece landed in our differential bodies: despite the appearance of consensus that an introduction (indeed an agreed upon table of contents) seems to espouse, we are editors with varied aesthetic and ethical preferences. And yet, there is an embodied response that comes from reading powerful poetry in a single room. Perhaps it's not as loud as the collective "va va shabash!" a room full of South Asian activists and lovers of poetry and music offer to a photograph of Umm Kulthum singing a Faiz Ahmed Faiz ghazal—projected via YouTube onto a daytime white wall—but it is loud, and it does have an air of the undeniable. The argument, of course, was also part of our process: the shift from head shake to head nod when a third read convinced one editor to transcend their tastes, the moments when either crucial content or divergent form demanded to invigorate the collection.

The poetic responses received for *Read America(s)* taught us how to make this anthology. Poems called to each other. For instance, major parts of the anthology were shaped by Elizabeth Acevedo's LHP 2015 Publication Prize winning poem "La Ciguapa," which calls forth resonant and contrapuntal poems such as Ishion Hutchinson's "A Surveyor's Journal," excerpts from Sherwin Bitsui's "Dissolve," and more. Similarly, Felix Mnthali's "Neocolonialism" converses with Angel Nafis' "Gravity" and Clifton Gachagua's "Cars." For us, this call-and-response resonates throughout the collection and helps it achieve some strange constellational balance.

We asked potential contributors to share their meditations: What is/are America(s)? What are its boundaries? Where is it? Is it real? What language does it speak? What stories does it tell?

Contributor responses expressed the America(s) of the mind, of physical space, of the body and bodies in and around it. The poets herein are often re-writing borders—borders of inclusion and exclusion, safety and danger, highly politicized existence, access to physical and emotional resources. Their "answers" are unique perceptions of pattern, and to build a response of them, a plucking of myriad stars out of the sky only to realize some identified as planets, indeed universes, of their own. The initial responses inspired LHP editors to explore further poems that seek to investigate the multiplicity of culture and identity that comprise a more inclusive and self-critical America(s), while simultaneously embracing the contradictions, the conflict and dysphagia associated with our efforts.

Another way we sought work that spoke to America(s) was to ask contributors of our past paired publications, *Read Women: An Anthology* and *Gendered & Written: Forum on Poetics*, who they identified as their literary ancestors and inspirations, many of whom are included here and whose inclusion shaped this text.

We were compelled to consider not only artists who identify as American, or whose geographical location places them in the Western Hemisphere, but those touched by America the colonizing, imperialist and cultural force. As we note above, an idea, especially one that is identified as, or de facto resonates with, empire, is not confined by the physical space it manifests. We needed ways to narrow our options that kept our wider vision. Although we kept Kofi Awoonor's "America"—a poem inceptive to this project, one that called and responded to so many poems herein—given that the manifestation of America(s) is a living, evolving experience, it made sense to focus on living writers.

Although we are certainly not the first to pluralize "America," or to question the name as it relates to global power structures and dominant ideology, we want to ask related questions via poems because poems are a more flexible way of understanding: What happens when you pluralize such a socially and historically complex entity? What happens when you complicate a dominant ideology? When you call it America(s) because there is not just one? In repeating these questions as editors to the text that follows, we cannot help but note that pluralizing "America" into America(s) is an incomplete methodology that inflects its own incompleteness. In returning to our core goal—to provide a space that opens poetic dialogue—we also note that *the poems* are finding ways toward a dynamic and compelling constellation-ized version that exceeds the name America(s).

We have come to terms as readers, and now as editors, that exhaustive texts do not exist and those that make such a claim are usually driven by the types of delusions that lead to colonial empire. What does exist is gesture, gesture against, towards, inside of and outward.

Above all, we hope this anthology demonstrates how so many contemporary artists work to challenge, gesture, dismantle and explore conflict while transforming it into art. As these poems manifest as a collection, our hope is that readers make out their own stories, find new constellations. We believe this possible, just as we believe all radical work, including the work of marginalized writers that express the complex experiences of strife, beauty, resistance, celebration, survival, place, thriving and messy conviviality, are essential to processing conflict, and deserve to be articulated, imagined and published.

    Hari Alluri and Amanda Fuller
    Locked Horn Press
    San Diego, Kumeyaay Land
    Turtle Island
    February 2016

POEMS

Elmaz Abinader

Heartwood

(As a tree grows, older xylem cells in the center of the tree become inactive and die, forming heartwood. Because it is filled with stored sugar, dyes and oils, the heartwood is usually darker than the sapwood. The main function of the heartwood is to support the tree.)

While you watch   you are being watched
and every word you write   is scribed on arm   henna
petrified with the veins of your witnessing.

You need to grow harder than fresh limbs
slick and sentient reaching and waiting.
Solidify the cambium harden your bark
capture your tears inside your trunk
molten tributaries moving with life—

What is seen are grandmothers
skimming barbed-wire
stuffing groceries under their skirts   scrambling over the gate
as you tick off one after another up and over   your jeep idles near the wall

The pinch of wire just refreshes old scars
they don't think as much of it as you do when

your organs soak with sugars
all the blood is trapped below
your heart. Even while it chokes you

the cells confine the color
drained from your face
as you watched them escape
to the other side of the same square of dust,   crippled tired
pulling on a power of healed-over wounds as thick as branches.

Examine those albino eyes
expressionless stupefyingly blind
and see in them rings of endless years

of stunted growth, roots lengthening below the terrain.

Where the heartwood thickens,   they have power
no one can see into the tree
where everything dead gathers and protects them
                                                       stone core wood heart.

Needlework
for Faith Adiele

1. LP

A needle drop
        one groove—aria:
        the mother's whalebone holler rocketing
        into mobsong: men in orange marched him onto the beach
a throat cut, bodies breathing beneath the sand, perforating

        singe to ear

this cymbal clatter, the rumble
              a collapsing not just the building, not just the home,
            the bones in parched pilings.

      We want to refuse   the blood soaked
terrain, the crack on the glass of his photograph;
his brother shaved close for the camera
        which is not different
from guerillas hacking the bush and then their backs

2. Tattoo

There is a chorus of ghost voices of girls lost
        puncturing in fine notes silhouettes
        where we pull scarves low to avert youth
        and beauty and still, again, stolen

seekers have lost their way or perhaps incentive
for what are girls but tiny birds fallen from nests?
Some forget but mothers woodcut faces over
the wombs where heartbeats flushed

3. Injection

I cannot seal my eyes or block my ears
my veins raise, easy to find when this one says
food, and another says, gas, and another says
my father burned before my eyes. Firecracker drones
celebrate their inability to distinguish farmer
from soldier, child from warrior. The warmth in the blood
breeds dissidents—flowing is dynamic, constant, poison
moves fast—a terrifying addiction

4. Acupuncture

Decorate me with needles. Stitch my mouth—
Embroider my forehead—give them all names
distinct as their laughter or the way eyes shied
even as they were gone

Pierce my chakras with their voices, run maps along
my meridians where they were last seen
alive, track my qi and extract elegy

I choose remembering
        it cuts
the skin
        impatient
morphs into the saddest stories ever told
again and again, and as small as this, we bleed
and scar and bleed again.

Elizabeth Acevedo

La Santa Maria
for Hispaniola

Leave that bitch at the bottom; wooden husk dulled and molded,
weighed with water. We don't need any more museums of white men.

Leave something for our black dead to play in. The bones of their once
brown bodies walking the Atlantic floor to dance around this first vessel.

We don't need Columbus' ship when he's already gifted us an ocean of ghosts—
imagine them in the thousands. Hundreds of thousands. Long released

from their skin crawling forward on an elbow, on a knee, knuckles, all gnaw.
Pressing eye-less skulls to the portholes. Knocking. Finally being let in to somewhere.

They stumble across the deck, touch the mottled curtains, spit on the iron fasteners,
place copper coins between the disks of their spines, dance.

I hope pirates have brushed fingers with these ghosts, that they've been led to all the gold
and pulled apart the ballast until it is nothing but a pile of splinters,

a great heap of wood meant to be left at the bottom; sell no tickets for this bringer
of apocalypses… but if, when you pull her up, you want to make a bonfire,

I've got the matches.

La Ciguapa
for the Antilles

They say La Ciguapa was born on the top of El Pico Duarte.
Balled up for centuries beneath the rocks,
she sprang out red, covered in boils, dried off black,
and the first thing she smelled was her burning hair.

•

They say Atabeyra carried La Ciguapa while in frog form—
held her low in the belly until squatting she laid her
into soft dirt: an egg made of ocean. Centuries later, La Ciguapa
poked through and the blue water burst and grafted onto her skin.

•

They say La Ciguapa pried apart her jaw
and spit herself out, soft and malleable,
but at the last second her legs scraped against
fangs and inverted her footing.

•

Her backwards-facing feet were no mistake, they say,
she was never meant to be found, followed—
an unseeable creature: crane legs, saltwater crocodile scales;
long beak of a parrot no music sings forth from.

•

La Ciguapa, they say, was made on one of those ships; stitched
and bewitched from moans and crashing waves. She emerged
entirely formed, dark and howling, stepped onto the auction
block but none would buy her. They wouldn't even look her in the eye.

•

They say she came beneath the Spanish saddle of the first mare.
Rubbed together from leather and dark mane. Hungry.

ACEVEDO

That she has a hoof between her thighs and loves men
like the pestle loves the mortar;

                                      she hums them into the cotton thick fog
of the mountains. They follow her none word nonsense
and try to climb her, tall and dark and rough as sugarcane
and don't know until they're whittled down how they've scraped

themselves dead. They say the men were the first to undo her name;
thinking burying it would rot her magic, that long cry
they were compelled to answer; they hung all five-toed dogs
because they alone knew her scent—

there was a time her silhouette shadowed the full moon, they say.

They say. They say. They say. Tuh, I'm lying. No one says. Who tells
her story anymore? She has no mother, La Ciguapa, and no children,
certainly not her people's tongues: we who have forgotten all our sacred monsters.

                  NOTE: Elizabeth Acevedo's "La Ciguapa" is the 2015 LHP Poetry Prize winner.

James E. Allman, Jr.

Orientation
after a Map of Isodore of Seville, c. 622

1.

A loaded word, but just a

word. In simpler times and terms, more about which direction
one faced. Facing correctly,
specifically, eastward—or

oriented—the east, or the Orient. Reoriented

from our contemporary perspective: neither right nor

left, our east or west, but upward or northward on the *mappae mundi.*
Orientem, oriens—the rising sun, the part of
the sky also where the sun rises every morning. Up, as if to imply
over our heads, and slips behind us in the evening time.
How literal and silly cartographers were

back then. Silly as toddlers. As a toddler boy who asks

a simple question: "When my eyes get bigger and bigger, will

I see the whole. World."

And his mother and father not knowing what he means,
supposing: *See it*
as it is. As topsy-turvy, turned upon its head, like those old maps
perhaps, which look remarkably as though they'd been drawn
by toddlers' hands: Their dependence on such thick lines.

2.

Thick black lines, but no longitude or latitude. Though we give them
a lot of latitude for being so simple-minded, such old men,

to think that the world was flat or carried once on a turtle's back—

our houses being houdahs, our Oriental carpets spun of

magic flax—or a cosmogonic egg,
cracked, poached, over easy or sunny-side up. Made to order. "Order up."

Silly as Quetzalcoatl or Pangu—moving heaven and earth for you

while walking on eggshells—calculating
Hubble's constant, constantly counting it out on

fingers and toes and expanding the poles of this
spheroid cosmos, according to one
ancient Chinese legend, like the ends of a breaking

egg separating—as a Big Bang, and as arcane.

3.

Or just plain arcane. Ancient,
archaic. *Archaeo-*, meaning olden or
from the beginning, like a rising up, *oriri*, to rise, or **ergh*,
similarly, raise or set in motion or stir.
Stirring, too, a beginning: And *styrian, *sturjanan, storan*—
to scatter or destroy—as much an
end as it is a beginning. As a storm is

also its own refreshment. Or the snake's consumption of

self is at the same moment a regurgitation of itself:
The Ouroboros, an ancient symbol. Or how the latest found fact of archeology

is simultaneously eschatology:
*the last writing being also
the first writing*, as in Alpha and Omega. Which is
why the aboriginal—*ab origine*, from the beginning,
originalis, origo—ever faced
the east, in the first place. In the first
place, which in the last place is why we find ourselves so disoriented. Turning

bigger and bigger telescopes: And so many suns in the sky.

Kofi Awoonor

America

A name only once
crammed into the child's fitful memory
in malnourished villages,
vast deliriums like the galloping foothills of the Colorado:
of Mohawks and the Chippewa,
horsey penny-movies
brought cheap at the tail of the war
to Africa. Where indeed is the Mississippi panorama
and the girl that played the piano and
kept her hand on her heart
as Flanagan drank a quart of moonshine
before the eyes of the town's gentlemen?
What happened to your locomotive in Winter, Walt,
and my ride across the prairies in the trail
of the stage-coach, the gold-rush and the Swanee River?
Where did they bury Geronimo,
heroic chieftain, lonely horseman of this apocalypse
who led his tribesmen across deserts of cholla
and emerald hills
in pursuit of despoilers,
half-starved immigrants
from a despoiled Europe?
What happened to Archibald's
soul's harvest on this raw earth
of raw hates?
To those that have none
a festival is preparing at graves' ends
where the mockingbird's hymn
closes evening of prayers
and supplication as
new winds blow from graves
flowered in multi-colored cemeteries even
where they say the races are intact.

SHERWIN BITSUI

> *from* **Dissolve**

Slipping into free-fall,
we drip-pattern
        the somewhere parts,

our shoulders dissolving
            in somewhere mud.

The arcing sun whistles
across the mask's abalone brow,
      its blurring pouts into a forest
          chirping from the lake's bite marks,
          stamped vertically
              on this map's windowsill.

Kneeling our thoughts on ellipses
        evaporating from ollas of fragrant wet clay—
           we saddle the drowning's slippery rim.

from **Dissolve**

What's left in our chests:
        scrapes teeth on bone meal.

Rented from a shepherd of doves
        we return   replenished with categories.

Dimmest below our downward gaze—
these stars
                gazing back at us.

Mario Bojórquez

A orillas del río Delaware frente a Camden y mirando las luces del Walt Whitman Bridge

Algún día te crecieron las barbas
como un río congelado
y te volviste hielo
viejo poeta cabeza de nube.

Por todo eso gritabas que México debía desaparecer
que el destino de tu nación era grande
tan grande que debía exterminar al mundo entero.

Algunos compatriotas tuyos
creyeron en tus palabras e intentaron tu sueño.

Aún hoy, a ciento cincuenta años de tu cólera
el rayo de mi lengua te canta en libertad.

Viejo, oh viejo, viejo, viejo Walt Whitman.

(1847-1997)

At the banks of the Delaware River Waterfront facing Camden and watching the lights of the Walt Whitman Bridge

One day you grew a beard
like a frostbitten river
and you turned to ice
ancient poet head of clouds

For all your screams that Mexico deserved to disappear
that the fate of your nation was large
so large it should exterminate the entire world

Some of your compatriots
believe in your words and tend your dream

—and today 150 years of your anger
the lightning of my tongue sings to you en libertad.

Old, old, old, viejo, viejo Walt
                      Whitman

(1847-1997)

Translated from the Spanish by Hari Alluri, Binh H. Nguyen and Jonathan Rodley

Museo Guggenheim

La incesante espiral por donde el mundo sube
                                           baja.
La espiral incesante por donde voy conmigo
                      para ascender en mi
                               y regresarme.

Por donde yo incesante
                       espiral de mis huesos.
Diestro desde lo mío
                hacia yo
      vuelta en mí mismo.

Incesante, por donde yo
                     espiral apenas.
Retorno sin aliento.

Espiral donde incesante yo
                       para mí, en mí.

Guggenheim Museum

The unceasing spiral where the world goes
                                below
The spiral unceasing where I go with me
                    to rise in myself
                            and return

For where I unceasing
                    spiral in my bones
Dextrous from what is mine
                        - around I
            twisting   in   myself

Unceasing where I
                only spiral
        breathless I
return

Where unceasing I spiral
                —toward me in me

Translated from the Spanish by Hari Alluri, Binh H. Nguyen and Jonathan Rodley

DANIEL BORZUTZKY

Dream Song #16

Hay golpes en la vida, tan fuertes… Yo no sé! — César Vallejo

They sniffed us out of the holes with the animals
they had programmed and there are blows in life so
powerful we just don't know and there were trenches
and there was water and it poured in through our mouths

and out of our ears and there were things we saw in the
sand at that moment of sinking: mountains and daisies
and tulips and rivers and the bodies of the people we
had been and the bodies of the people we had loved

and we felt hooks coming through the trenches and we
felt hooks coming through the sand and I saw hooks coming
through my child's clothes and I wanted him to know that they
would never be able to scoop us out of the sand but of course

it wasn't true they had scooped us out of the sand and our
mouths were so full of dirt it is what they do when you're
dead and they made us spit and they beat us until our mouths
were empty and they paid us for constructing the mountain and

it was me and L and we looked for S and we looked for J and J
and we looked for O and we looked for R and we looked for J
and S in the holes in which the bodies of those we loved were
hiding or dying or sinking or stealing some shelter some little

worm's worth of cover to keep their bodies from dissolving
into the maniac murmurs of this impossible carcass economy

Geoff Bouvier

Invitation Only

It always starts with a party in someone's pants. There's a party of one. Sooner or later, you or I become a party to the party. We throw the periodic house party. Our neighbors come together for the monthly block party. Our city holds a festival throughout the city, yearly. There is dancing in the street. The states take holidays. Our bankers unite, and recover. History takes holidays. Dead people reanimate into memory. The country has its birthday. Our workers unite, and recover. But there's never any parties between countries. Parties larger than the countries are called wars.

The Paradox of the Heap of Troubles

It's Monday, remove that expression of joy.

Mondays, minus those million-dollar smirks.

Monday, subtracting the winning teams, the losing teams, your channels devoted, everyone a morning quarterback.

Today the glad hands come out, our mutual reach, beyond blue bins of garbage at the curbs. Monday, no recycling.

Monday, hum along, hum of human and mechanism. Begin the commute and accumulate.

Monday, Monday, pile up cares, add the blues and sing through tears.

Monday, you're doing it wrong.

Mondays, voices, dollars, votes. Monday, a gabfest destiny. Monday, taxing your final security.

Monday, Monday, heaps of sand, disappearing grain by grain.

Another corporate day, another put down demonstration, the aim at armament, the masculinity. The monolith, the monument. The city, from gutter to spire, inhabitant and squatter, well-regarded by tourists.

Any Monday minus the cop shooting. Monday, minus ruinous shorelines, tanked on oil. Monday, plus or minus our guns.

Monday, Monday, piece by piece, the trouble's never any less.

What day is it? A machine has a baby, crying engine clatter, steal away the stun-grenade inside the crib. I flip my egg, it breaks. All right, kids, take notes.

Every Monday, can't get a do-over. Every Monday, can't get a haircut. Every Monday, the newsworthy backlash, minus flashing gunmetal, minus a shooting of innocents, plus the person who talks to you and makes you feel smart, plus the person who talks to you and makes you feel heard.

Every Monday, an investment scam, a pyramid scheme, a sham election. Here's indifference for your troubles, here's a shamwow for your tears.

Every five minutes, a man is worth a dollar. Every five minutes, a woman's worth seventy-seven cents. Boiling frogs on slippery slopes.

Any day, minus my voice, my vote. A wall of separation between education and state. Any day, class is in session. Class struggles. Class is in trouble.

Every day, we justify evil in the name of faith. Every moment is a test of our voices. Every year, there's a test of our votes. Every day is a test of dollars. Every day, the globe is warming up to us.

Everyday troubles grow too slowly for urgency. Every day on the heap of too slow emergencies.

DERRICK WESTON BROWN

Despite

for Sunil Tripathi, of Brown University, who was named a suspect in the April 2013 Boston Marathon Bombing by Reddit although he had been missing since mid-March. His body was found nearly two weeks later, and for Salah Eddin Barhoum, an unnamed "Saudi Man," and "Brown Running Man," and all those who fit a description.

Your brown skin is not a bomb.
Your brown skin does not mean bomb.
Though they doctor pictures.
Though they cry cowards.
Though drones may have your name on rolodex.
Though they *cry why do they hate us so*, with the ball of their foot on your neck.
Though they stop and frisk.
Though they shun background checks.
Though they throw stones and hide their hands.
Though they stroke gun butts.
Though they fondle sleek barrels in their sleep.
Though they run their hands through shotgun shells like loose grain.
Though their journalism is pale and piss colored.
Though they peer through their own monstrous veil.
Though they forget home grown rotted roots.
Though they pull weeds and crush seeds in others' gardens.
Though they flash your photos with reckless intent.
Though they posse up.
Though they scramble like keystone cops.
Though they shoot first.
Though they shoot first.
Your brown skin is not a bomb.
Your brown skin does not mean bomb.
Your breath is good mornings.
Your eyes are promises backed by
prayers uttered from the backs of throats
of those who love first and question later.
Your brown skin is a country
unblemished
free.

Halle Tells How They Broke Him
from The Sweet Home Men Series
for Toni Morrison

Let me tell you something. A man ain't a goddamn ax.
Chopping busting every goddamn minute of the day!
Things get to him. Things he can't chop down because
they're inside!
—Paul D

I.

Churn

Churn

My brains is soured
all the rich gone.

What is left
that they ain't already taken?

Think you got say-so
they break they neck to prove

different. Prayer ain't mine
either. Money never been mine.

Best I ever did besides
Sethe and the babies was

working my fingers to
the gristle to buy my own mama
a clear path.

II.

Curdle

Curdle

When things get thick

D. Brown

you add milk
to get the thin

Add milk for righteous biscuits

Sweet cream to the cornmeal

Add milk to cull the heat out a burn

Milk is life and

they took
they took
they took.

Call me anything but a Man.

What is a man if his hands can't
hold on to something
build something
plant chop cook crop kill reap?

Man ain't suppose to hide,
to thief, steal away.
A man supposed to do.

What you do when they
cut your hands off with no knife?

What you do when they
steal the run in your legs?

Sixo say we made of things
stronger than what fills they
skins.

But where they learn
how to break us in places
we can't see?

D. Brown

Wrap our song up in
their fists then beat us with it?

III.

It's like they know
when you get close
to heaven and they
smell it and they move
they see the dance in
your eyes and they
read it word for word
they smell the sweet
and they want it for them
selves and they ease in
like air like a corn snake
and they snatch it and rip
it open like they did my
Sethe's shirt and cut
a chokecherry tree
on her oak brown back
with a beast's skin flayed
and worn and wicked
and them boys
them mossy teeth boys
rolled her on her back
suckled like two pale piglets
and their grunts
turned my brains
to porridge and I
couldn't do nothing
couldn't cry out
cause they don't
deserve to hear my
pain that's for Sethe
only only she didn't
make a sound but her
eyes was searching
wet and wide and

D. Brown

those eyes went
back to iron and
I wanted
I wanted
to make
a trench
of their heads
with a shovel
but my spine
is butter

my heart has curdled
my brain is clabber
and my babies have no
milk and I can't run
with no spine
where can I go
where they can't take
my babies milk or
me or mama cause
they took my mind when
they took Sethe
and I saw
I saw I saw I saw
and the sour got in me
and stayed and
call me anything but
a man.

IV.

This is where my mind
smeared thick and sticky
churned and curdled
call me anything
call me anything
but.

Jericho Brown

On Daniel Minter's High John the Conqueror

The sun inflicts its whitest light, heat
High enough to warp the pavement,
So John gives up on the new road north
And cuts through red clay at first sight
Of shade, barbed wire broken, miles
Of green to be cleared or cleaned growing
In rows like welts behind him. God's
Not on his side. John won't work
A whole day and can't keep cancer
Out his mouth. Oh, he's got the shoulders
For it, the stride, arms and hands
The size of a laboring man's, but one
Itch for smoke in his throat and John
Heads for hell. Nothing about Georgia
Can slow him down. King of all
That slithers, here he chokes a snake.
I catch his yellow eye and remember
My own pack of menthols, days I'd drag
And puff lies in front of my wife who
Waited while I wished for man after man,
Black in two dimensions, to run my way,
Dear John, a region painted against me.

J. Brown

Layover

Dallas is so far away
Even for the people who live
In Dallas is Dallas far away
A hub
Through which we get
To smaller places
That lurch and hurt
Mean stopping
In Dallas and all are
From small towns and farms
If all keep going
Back far enough
Pay attention
Keep your belongings near
Everyone in Dallas
Is still driving
At 3:24 a.m. off I-20
Where I was raped
Though no one
Would call it that
He was inside
By the time I realized
He thought it necessary
To leave me with knowledge
I can be hated
I was smaller then
One road went through me
No airport
I drove him home
There had been a wreck
On the interstate
I sat in traffic
My wallet on the seat
In between my legs.

Alí Calderón

from **Constantinopla**

                [San Salvador en Chora]

Edirnekapi
Siglo IV una iglesia bizantina
Afuera las murallas de Teodosio
son sólo polvo ruinosos cimientos
Iba mi abuelo anciano
siempre a Nuestra Señora del Carmen a las once
¿comulgaba? ¿Oía sólo misa?
La luz de los vitrales cae sobre los frescos:
es Jesús
multiplica los panes
hay algunos pescados
también cestas vacías
Alguien a mi costado dice "Dios"
pero en el nártex nada suena sino el eco
bajo la indiferencia
de un Cristo Pantocrátor
El tiempo ha desgastado los cristales
diminutos mosaicos
Donde estuvo el Bautista se desvela
una capa de arena y argamasa
El muro fue dorado y lapislázuli
ahora el alquitrán
oculto quince siglos
tras figuras de apóstoles y santos
es amo y señor del paraclesion.
Bordean yeso y cal oscuros signos
griegos: venid a mí los agobiados
dicen las inscripciones
difusas
invisibles casi
Las cuarteaduras
Se descascaran bóvedas
frente a la sanación del paralítico
Los ladrillos la piedra
Es entonces que pienso en los versos finales:
Mi padre contestó –"eso es sólo el decorado;
la escultura eres tú" –y me señaló el pecho.

Calderón

from Constantinopla

        [The Church of St. Salvador of Chora]

Edirnekapi: Four centuries ago a Byzantine Church
Outside the walls of Theodosius:
concrete & ruins & dust.
My grandfather always
at Our Lady of Carmen at eleven
reflecting? listens to mass?
Light falls from windows upon frescos.
It's Jesus.
Multiplying loaves of bread. Jesus.
There are fish.
Empty baskets. Jesus.
Someone by my side says, "God"
But what is at the entrance? Nothing. But is nothing? Echoing sounds.
Under indifference
of a Christ Pantocrator
Time has worn the glass
like tiny mosaics
The Baptist reveals
a layer of sand & mortar
the wall is gold and lapis
Now tar.
Hidden for fifteen centuries behind statues of apostles & saints
Love & lord of paraclesion
Lime plaster & dark border signs
Written in Greek: come to me, hurried, overwhelmed—
Inscriptions almost invisible
Diffuse
the cracks
vaults are scaled
stone bricks
Opposite of healing the lame, opposite of lame, the paralyzed
Opposite of what I think is the final verse—
My father answers—"this is only decoration"
"You are the sculpture"—& I pointed toward my chest

Translated from the Spanish by Ana Bosch and Karla Cordero

[Kentucky]

Las luces cambiaron en West Vine y Broadway Street
el viento helado amortajó la tarde
volando un grajo sajó la transparencia
y la luz en las hojas
el trazo de finos pinceles parecía

En el aire altísimo
la claridad del día
supuso una presencia.

Calderón

[Kentucky]

The light changes in West Vine & Broadway Street
The cool wind stashes the afternoon
A flying crow cuts through transparency
& the light on the leaves

—the fine strokes of brushes appeared
in high wind souring
of day's clarity:
supuso una presencia
whispers us into present

Translated from the Spanish by Ana Bosch and Karla Cordero

Grady Chambers

Lake Shore Limited, Hour Seventeen

I couldn't sleep and I'd lost a lens. So half the passing landscape
        was the amber of a shaded eye, half the white wash
of ordinary daylight. And I wanted something to bless.
        But Indiana came and went and Ohio passed by like a stutter:
churchyard. Churchyard. Vine-veined brick. Burnt-orange boxcars
        stacked like Rothkos. Smoke from a smile
of teardrop trailers scattered through the trees. And a shuttered garage
        howled out from its abandoned face: that I have never known
silence or the solitude of real country. That America is woodsmoke
        and breath and vastness, the church of the boarded
factory, sunset driven through its throat. That we need to live more locally,
        small and homegrown and humble. That territorial integrity
is a precursor to violence. And wilderness is a question of proximity.
        That ways of life are dying. And we live in a secular time. And I fear
I will be the only passenger on this route in 30 years.
        That the long dawns of winter, when the sun
makes dying coals of the cloud banks and the sky's progression is of ash
        to blue to sullied white, is better than the summer dawn's blood-
sun scalding the horizon. Likewise that beaches are more beautiful in winter,
        their blue and silver moonscapes. That the forest, too, is a kind of altar,
and the golden rows of grassland are its paths. That the wind-blown
        mists of snow are equally worthy of worship.
And each little river we roll over as holy as blood.

Dispatch: Bamyan, Helmand, Baghlan, Ghor, 2008

In high school we squinted at the grainy film
of a beheading and watched the glow of televised mortars in Iraqi cities,
discussed body counts and tactics, fired up the console to a pixilated warfare
where a gentle hand was prized in rolling a grenade beneath an enemy tank.
    We cheered when one another's screens went red.
And we talked about God, Rachmaninoff, the battleships docked
off Pakistan and the Afghan Provinces: *Bamyan, Helmand, Baghlan, Ghor.*
We spoke the names like we'd been there.
    While Ryan went to basic training on Parris Island we watched
on television our leaders' claims of victory, behind them the unseen losses, the
blacked out boxes wrapped in flags and stacked in cargo holds and delivered to a
cemetery in Arlington.
You'd have to travel a thousand miles and a day to understand the weight
of bodies staring up at their own flagged headstones.
    I never did. Instead I walked
through an airport with a closely cropped head and a duffel and was stopped
by a woman who touched my chest and said *thank you, thank you
for your service.*
    I did not correct her. I walked away
and was later embarrassed sitting in a gilded library where I wrote papers on the
ethics of war and torture and watched Ryan's status updates change from *Parris!*
to *0500 for laps at Shutter Island*, to *balls deep in recon county*,
to pictures where men—boys really—stood in lines gripping guns in a vertical hold.
    Then silence,
then Ryan sunglassed and kneeling in camo, smoke rising off the road: he had
turned
into an abstract specific—Machine Gunner, CAB, 4th Marines—while I clicked
refresh, refresh, until he returned home on leave and we sat in a bar
and I looked at his chest—the thickness, the flatness—
and talked about the elections while he shrugged and nodded.
    The distance
was in the scraps of labels I'd peeled off bottles, the silence
in the book of war stories I inscribed with a Schopenhauer quote about human
suffering and gave him before his second tour and later found beneath the passenger
seat of my car.
    And the silence is in the way my heart beats
the memory of the day a cell phone lit up a vest

that turned a market in Helmand to fragments
and bodies back to atoms
and Ryan's status changed to *RIP PFC Dustin Bray, feels like yesterday
I was bumming Cope off you in the barracks, Semper Fi,*
the same day my friends and I lit bottle rockets on rooftops
and called each other
by our idiot nicknames—Slick Pesos, Donny Rubble, Frankie Knuckles—
and jammed our hands into foam fingers,
and cheered in a stadium
at the ceremony of F-16s tearing seams in the sky.

Nadia Chaney

Physical Education Grade Six
Great Slave Lake, Alberta, Canada

"many of our students ask about handguns
so we have included this section although
it should be understood that handguns
are not legal or useful for the purpose of hunting
    animals"

    bitter winter skin
    thin and unforgiving
    what is living is hardened
    into stillness for a season

alone in a classroom with
a new box of textbooks
stamped Alberta Dept of Ed

socks flop on the green tile floor
my wet footprints follow me

flip illustrations
of white kids
in black outline
playing badminton
and heart smart

a chapter on hunting:
how to shoot, skin, smoke and
preserve the face for trophy

the icy wind

Wintering Place
Alaska Highway, km 765

motel receptionist:

the furniture wears
his moustache
gray rough trimmed red
plaid crumbs and change

he wears its wood paneled walls
across his chest in sad armour
their dingy trophies
with all bared teeth
       cougar, elk and blacktail deer

says we can have the attic if we're game

a long weekend here;
       I love the quiet you say
         drumming on the counter
         rattling antler pens and
         maple leaf lapel pins

across the road
the sunset fuschia
is a tinting bath
for your skin and clothes

you stuff tufts of fur
from a soft strewn hill
into your pockets

last week
you tied a big bone
   with fishing line and leather
to our van

set a tiny wooden piano in the trunk
   always in danger of being crushed

by our baggage
        (delicate better broken or
you melody fractal
self-existing
as the   (moon
crosses the horizon

the pine sentry outline
cold overseeing
nibbling into my collar

a black eye: a wood bison
sloping face
brown hair long and curl tipped
short spire of horn
under the blue church
of the watching

        bison crossing
        we wait here
        his right of way
        unvictorious but
        indomitable
        inverting
        we become the ghosts

waiting in history the last herd
rebounding along this river,
leaving their smell in seasons
this one
        wide
                eye

      silent, I confess our bone to that eye
and the soft stolen hair in your pockets

back at the lodge
room

desk and fat
old keys
unmoved

in my dream
a black hair river

in the morning
the bone is gone

Jennifer Chang

This Corner of the Western World

Dark thing,
make a myth of yourself:

all women turn into lilacs,

all men grow sick of their errant scent.
You could learn

to build a window, to change flesh
into isinglass, nothing

but a brittle river, a love of bone.

You could snap like a branch—*No,*

this way, he says, and the fence
releases the forest,

and every blue insect finds an inch of skin.
He loves low voices, diffidence

on the invented trail,

the stones you fuck him on. Yes
to sweat's souvenir, yes to his fist

in your hair, you bite

because you can. Silence
rides the back of your throat,

his tongue, your name.

BRICEIDA CUEVAS COB

U áak' abil tuchibil uj

In xch'upul aal,
ch'ik púutso'ob ti' a nook',
tak a xchak eex,
uk' u xp'o'oja'il ka'
yo'olal ma' u p'atik u yuuy xma uj
tu wíinklil a chaampal
ken a la'achabaj.

U áak'abil tu chibil uj.
U áak'abil ka laj p'u'uj peek'o'ob u tak' u jajawchi'ibalo'ob ti' ch'e'eneknakil.
U áak'abil tu yáakan ju'ob.
Le tu máan yáalkab máako'ob tumen ts'o'ok u jaanta'al xma uj.

Ichil ek'joch'e'enil
juntúul ko'olel,
u jach xyo'omil ichil u láak' xyo'omo'ob;
leti'e' ma' tu ch'ikaj puts'o'ob tu nook',
leti'e' ma' tu takaj u xchak eex
mix tu yuk'aj u xp'o'o ja'il ka';
leti'e' tu la'achaj u wolisil u neek' u yich yo'olal u seen booxtal u neek' u yich u paal,
tu luk'aj xma uj,
le tuun tu kaxanij uj tumen máako'ob ku páakato'ob ti' ka'an,
ko'olel tu sáaskunaj ich kaaj yéetel sáasil ku k'itik u chuun u nak'.

Night of the Eclipse

> *Daughter,*
> *fasten pins to your clothes,*
> *put on red panties,*
> *drink the water that washed the metate*
> *so that mother moon will not leave her mark*
> *on the body of your children*
> *when you scratch yourself.*

Night of the eclipse.
Night when the dogs tattooed their barking on the silence.
Night of the groaning conches.
When the people ran because they had eaten mother moon.

In the dark,
a woman,
most pregnant among the pregnant;
one who fastens no pins,
one who wears no red panties,
who never drinks the water that washed the metate;
one who scratched her eyes so that the eyes of her children would be blackest,
she swallowed the moon,
and while everyone looked for the moon in the sky,
the woman lit up the village with the light her belly spilled.

Translated from Maya via Spanish as an intermediary by Carolann Caviglia Madden

In k'aaba'

In k'aaba'e',
tikin oot'el,
chi'il chi' u chi'ichi'al,
u cha'acha'al tumen u ts'a'ay máako'ob.
Ts'o'ok in pitik u nook'il in k'aaba'
je' bix u pots'ikubal kaan tu xla' sóol.
¿Báanten ma' táan u ya'ala'al xkáakbach ti' uj?
Leti'e' suuk u xíinbal bul áak'ab,
suuk u bulik u wíinklil,
suuk u balik u su'utal,
suk u t'ubkubaj ich eek'joch'e'enil tumen ts'o'ok
u p'ektik u sáasil.
Tumen leti'e' sak ki'ichpan xba'aba'al.
In k'aba'e'
cha' ta'aka'an ti' paalal.
Bejla'e' mina'an in k'aaba'.
Tene' aluxen táan in so'oso'ok't'ik u tso'otsel u pool yaamaj.

My Name

My name,
skin flayed,
from mouth to mouth, bitten,
chewed by the eyeteeth of the people.
I have stripped the clothes of my name,
like a snake shedding skin.
Why not call the moon a whore?
She usually walks at night, is
used to betting on her body, is
used to concealing sin, is used
to diving in darkness
to avoid her light.
Because she is a pretty white pest.
My name is gum
that children can't have.
Now I have no name.
I am a duende who knots the hair of love.

Translated from Maya via Spanish as an intermediary by Carolann Caviglia Madden

Karla Cordero

This skin be

born from wolf womb.
bowls of blood moon.

bone know crow sob.
know moss mouth.

know cop look.
know oak cross.

blooms body into
ghost fog. cold box tomb.

fold. absolve.   poof.
now jukebox dove song.

 howl home god. howl home.

El Rancho '92

I see a country in each eye—as her
hand & comb rack through my scalp—loose strands

far from reach—like Mexico. Aqua sprays.
Tightening my ponytail, she tells stories of where milk is goat

utter fresh & chickens
bless the farm in eggs full of babies lost & feather.

El rancho, she says, *is where the sun splits open
sky to burn cornfields gold, brushes the onion*

leaves, & pigs carcass their way back to earth. I remember
my young tongue ask, *when can the goats & chickens visit?*

Petra's black hair sweeps across her back—
the perfume of desert dust still caught in

a mountain between here & motherhood—
Never, she says, *they're busy feeding my children's bellies.*

Cynthia Cruz

Sparks, Nevada

In the middle of the night, father
Brought me a falcon.

By morning, it ripped the wire and flew the hill
Into the highway.

When they found me in that car
My sleeve stemmed in blood,

I didn't know what it was
I was trying to kill.

I saw a craft of orphans steaming down the river.
They were dressed in white and silent as a séance.

It was then I spoke to the bird.

Already God is shaking his black seed
Back into me.

Twelve in Yellow-Weed at the Edge

Then, the police arrive—they don't find me.
I'm disguised as a boy in a champagne wig
And hid inside the gold rattle of a warm Appalachia wind.
Beneath the trash of willow, I am. The sorrow
Of trailer parks and carnie uncles. The poor
Girl's underworld, a weedy thing. The night,
With its kingdom of lanterns and awful blue lark.
How we waited, how we hid
Like wolves, in the revolving question of a field.

Kyle Dargan

Looking East as a Man Repairs Lights on the South Street Pier
I too lived—Brooklyn, of ample hills, was mine
— Walt Whitman, "Crossing the Brooklyn Ferry"

From this low perch, I cannot identify
who is a hipster. Supposedly, they have
colonized everything out there—beyond
the far bank of this busy brown river.

So many buildings have felt wrecking
(via ball, via plane) since I spent odd afternoons
as a boy upon this pier, waiting for water's
interpretation of our lives. (We being
mostly water, I assumed a river might know.)

    Still, the shadow of the bridge
and Whitman's words make a humble shroud.
If not the world, at least the America's
meaning spoke clearest to me here—
under this iron and stone span
twenty-seven men perished to erect.

Ellis Island wades downriver
somewhere we can't see, can't recall.
Crossing, constant crossing.
Cross or be crossed. No malice in that—
either you're crossing a line in this land
our becoming the line to be traversed.

    Between the pier
and the water, only a railing. An electrician
hooks his harness to the metal, then hops
over the side to replace broken lights.
He is fearful of falling in the river, of losing
his place in this country. He knows
the boundaries we've imagined, we've drawn,
have no authority beneath the water
—its undulating disregard for the ink,
the shading, we think defines us.

China Cycle XI: "Beautiful Country"

The hanzi for "hai" (海) I decipher from expressway
signs above us as we depart the new Port of Binhai.

I ask Dongxia what "Shanghai" then means.
"No meaning. When it is name, it is just name."

I struggle to digest her response, having realized
the phrasing of Mandarin's myriad characters

harbors the figurative—how "holy" as hanzi
stacks the character for "other" atop the tree-like

character for "earth," resculpting the metaphor
in calligraphy (圣). I show Dongxia my strokes

for a character that's caught my eye (京) to ask,
again, for translation. "This means Beijing—

one character." But "bei" I've now memorized
as "north." I follow my finger through my book

until it catches on "jing": "capital." North Capital.
Beijing—as much a name as a geographical

distinction. Later, I glean "shang" (上) off street
signs near my lodging. I open the dictionary

which confesses it means "up," maybe "upper."
Upper Port. Shanghai. North of Hong Kong.

(There was a Duke of an old English York,
I plan to tell Dongxia. The York that now cradles

Manhattan is the New. I seek similar backstory
when I ask what hides behind the hanzi's blades.)

Before I fancy myself a sleuth of language
here in the Middle Nation (中国), I must learn

what I mean in Mandarin. After calling myself
"Mei Guo" (美国) for weeks, I realize that

it can't be simply "America." The book confides
that "mei" means beautiful, that I am "ren"

(人) from the Beautiful Country. I moan,
heavy. The translation can't be right—how

do I explain all the beauty not found there?

Meg Day

Teenage Lesbian Couple Found in Texas Park with Gunshot Wounds to the Head
Portland, Texas | June 24, 2012

It's always the girls   (we girls)
who mistake our heartbeats for hammers—
suffer their pounding when your kindness
insists it requires no exchange, & hush
their racket when a few rounds with Captain
or Jack change your mind, training us like dogs
to flinch every time you raise a hand.

It's always the girls   (we girls)
who wake with more Adam in our step
than Eve, who weave back & forth
with intention, or wear our hair & lashes long
for anyone that is not you; who try Pleases, try tears, try Jesus
                      but still pop up in pairs along Colonial Parkway
                      & in Medford, our bonds made literal & eternal
                      in truck stop restrooms & along the Appalachian Trail.

It's always the girls
who assume we'll outlast your barbed wire
boundaries our bodies hurdle on the daily,
convinced our steel jaws will be found intact
when authorizes, or archaeologists, unearth
each grave you chose for burying your rage
alongside our bodies, still intertwined.

SUNSHINE DEMPSEY

Tiresias in Love

     you can't   *(cannot)*   *speak it.*
                — Diodorus Siculus

            (let's have a frank talk, darling)

when Tiresias wakes up on Monday : begins the banalities of the morning

: returns from the mountains and searches for ticks thinking only
of the parasite and the blood and the host and the body: thinking of machinery

walking   along the way came a group of children playing with a bicycle
toward me on the sidewalk she asked me if I was a boy or a girl and I told her
I was & then upon my return again passed the children & a boy
asked was I a boy or a girl. and I told him yes. and then I went home.

   what if, with desperation,   *biform? only to*

            encase my heart, dearest one.

  these are little shadow boxes I am to be twain and so undone.

when I drink my coffee in the morning I am neither one nor t'other. just a one
concerned with temperature & where I've placed my lighter or a certain stack of
    papers or if
the air conditioner will freeze up

I think there is the tiniest of windows now I think I could catch (the neutered

noun) for you tangible:
    a *monstrosity*.

    how is this word to be received?

Tiresias sits at the end of a long bar and chain smokes. beautiful in form but
    lurking.
an untouchable creation, thus busted: making Haphaestus blush above
    Birmingham

    I am diapason I am so physical I am trans-lucent.
    o how I will pass
    as many times as you: trust me:

        to be regarded as a member of the biological present:

considering another name
standing barefoot on the linoleum in baggy grey trunks
: surveys the apartment and finds it the mausoleum of summer or more
a matter of grammar. a problem
of grammar: a noun and then   not a noun

                (a trans-itive)

it can be difficult to sentence:
 (what we have to do is build up and then dismantle   how we're trained in form
    and frame)

always asked to choose a shore

swimming in the ocean by the gulf: one becomes the oyster-littered water
the green chop water
beneath an oncoming storm.

calling out:
                          I am in love o   let me be this, love, o take these words away

one tries to choose the right side but always *Are you : are You?*

Yes—we are.

what great love there is in this body,
what great fear to look to the depths and see a handsome thing : unmitigated.

hold hard and gentle this frame,
this softly skeined bone

                    I give you this the sum : both to one, not the shores
                                   but the sea between me.

Natalie Diaz

Other Small Thundering

We are born with spinning coins in place of eyes,
paid in full to ferry Charon's narrow skiffs.
    we red-cloaked captains helming dizzying
       fits of sleep. Tied to the masts,
not to be driven mad by the caroling of thirsty children
or the symphony of dogs slaking hunger
by licking our ribcages like xylophones.
Our medicine bags are anchored with buffalo nickels—
    sleek skulls etched by Gatlings.
How we plow and furrow the murky Styx, lovingly
digging with smooth dark oars—
    like they are Grandmother's missing legs—
        a familiar throb of kneecap, shin, ankle, foot—
    promising to take us home.

A gunnysack full of tigers wrestles in our chests—
    they pace, stalking our hearts, building a jail
    with their stripes. Each tail a fuse. Each eye a cinder.
Chest translates to bomb.
Bomb is a song—
    the drum's shame-hollowed lament.
Burlap is no place for prayers or hands.
The reservation is no place for a jungle.
    But our stomachs growl. Somewhere within us
    there lies a king, and when we find him…

The snow-dim prairies are garlanded with children—
    my people dance circles around pyres but do not
    celebrate the bodies, small, open, red as hollyhocks.
Some crawled until they came undone—
    petal by petal,
    stripping the white field crimson.
Others lay where they first fell, enamored by the warmth
of a blanket of blood.
My dress is bluer than a sky weeping bones—
    so this is the way to build a flag—
        with a pretty little Springfield .45 caliber rifle.

So this is the way to sew wounds—
        with a hot little Howitzer.

Yesterday is much closer than today—
    a black bayonet carried between the shoulder blades
    like an itch, or the bud of a wing.
We've memorized the way a Hotchkiss can wreck a mouth.
Streetlights glow, neon gourds, electric dandelions—
    blow them out!
Wish hard for orange buttes and purple canyons,
moon-hoofed horses with manes made from wars,
other small thundering.

A Woman with No Legs
for Lona Barrackman

Plays solitaire on TV trays with decks of old casino cards   Trades her clothes for faded nightgowns long & loose like ghosts   Drinks water & Diet Coke from blue cups with plastic bendy straws   Bathes twice a week   Is dropped to the green tiles of her HUD home while her daughters try to change her sheets & a child watches through a crack in the door   Doesn't attend church services cakewalks or Indian Days parades   Slides her old shoes under the legs of wooden tables & chairs   Lives years & years in beds & wheelchairs stamped "Needless Hospital" in white stencil   Dreams of playing kick-the-can in asphalt cul-de-sacs below the brown hum of streetlights about to burn out   Asks her great-grandchildren to race from one end of her room to the other as fast as they can & the whole time she whoops Faster! Faster!   Can't remember doing jackknifes or cannonballs or breaking the surface of the Colorado River   Can't forget being locked in closets at the old Indian school   Still cries telling how she peed the bed there   How the white teacher wrapped her in her wet sheets & made her stand in the hall all day for the other Indian kids to see   Receives visits from Nazarene preachers Contract Health & Records nurses & medicine men from Parker who knock stones & sticks together & spit magic saliva over her   Taps out the two-step rhythm of Bird dances with her fingers   Curses in Mojave some mornings   Prays in English most nights   Told me to keep my eyes open for the white man named Diabetes who is out there somewhere carrying her legs in red biohazard bags tucked under his arms   Asks me to rub her legs which aren't there so I pretend by pressing my hands into the empty sheets at the foot of her bed   Feels she's lost part of her memory the part the legs knew best like earth   Her missing kneecaps are bright bones caught in my throat

CAMILLE DUNGY

'Tis of thee, sweet land (a poem of found text)

I tremble for my country when I remember God is just.

•

                    keep a sharp look out
                              under trap doors or in attic crawl spaces

                        50,000 fugitives found shelter
not far from where they took a glass of brandy

    pistols and bowie knives
    suddenly become scarce in the market

the padlock and chain were left in the woods

•

raised corn and cotton and cane and 'taters and goobers

    then along came a Friday and that a unlucky star day

    we have been at some great pains to ascertain the facts

•

    the institution is destined to become extinct
    at some distant day
    the wells have in some places dried up
    and the supplies of many mill streams have been much reduced

    the public are hereby cautioned against trusting or giving credit to any person

about Richmond
the locusts abound
they have cast their old shells and are depositing their eggs

                they have been heard to say blood must be shed

There Are Seven Things I Know, And None of Them Is You

How to fast lace a boot
so the tongue is close.
So nothing is left loose.
So I can walk. So I can run.

How to run.

How to speak the words and numbers
that signify where I belong.
How to count the houses.
How to walk inside a room.
How to find the bed I'll sleep in.

How to know I am not home.

Jesus Antonio Esparza

A Hum Falling from Mi Abuela's Mouth

This country burns—

      tiny ash tornadoes swirl at my feet.

Calluses thick in my palm—

      pit of a quarter flipped

against the edge of a bullet head—

      hole-punched faux picket fence,

avocados turned inside-out

      drowned in lime juice, burnt lip chipped mouth of a *molcajete*.

Mi abuela hums—

      a zipper stitched over his face, the sound of a boy's new skin.

Jill Alexander Essbaum

I Am Most Myself

When dispossessed.
When lost or impossible.
When I'm fraudulent
Or automaton-ish.

When almost a trauma.
When Christly. When cross.
When little lamb lostly.
When just because.

When I'm a pauper.
When I'm a laundress.
When first incautious,
Then applauded.

And when in August
I'm accosted.
When apostolic.
When exhausted.

When in peril.
When post-coital.
When I'm a ghost.
When I'm in hell.

When a grizzled laugh
Onslaughts.
When pissed up.
When fucked off.

And when in a black room
I'm attacked
By that old, stone sadness
And I don't fight back.

Tarfia Faizullah

100 Bells

with thanks to Vievee Francis

My sister died. He raped me. They beat me. I fell
to the floor. I didn't. I knew children,
their smallness. Her corpse. My fingernails.
The softness of my belly, how it could
double over. It was puckered, like children,
ugly when they cry. My sister died
and was revived. Her brain burst
into blood. Father was driving. He fell
asleep. They beat me. I didn't flinch. I did.
It was the only dance I knew.
It was the kathak. My ankles sang
with 100 bells. The stranger
raped me on the fitted sheet.
I didn't scream. I did not know
better. I knew better. I did not
live. My father said, I will go to jail
tonight because I will kill you. I said,
She died. It was the kathakali. Only men
were allowed to dance it. I threw
a chair at my mother. I ran from her.
The kitchen. The flyswatter was
a whip. The flyswatter was a flyswatter.
I was thrown into a fire ant bed. I wanted to be
a man. It was summer in Texas and dry.
I burned. It was a snake dance.
He said, Now I've seen a Muslim girl
naked. I held him to my chest. I held her
because I didn't know it would be
the last time. I threw no
punches. I threw a glass box into a wall.
Somebody is always singing. Songs
were not allowed. Mother said,
Dance and the bells will sing with you.
I slithered. Glass beneath my feet. I
locked the door. I did not
die. I shaved my head. Until the horns
I knew were there were visible.
Until the doorknob went silent.

Katie Farris

What We See in the Dark

"This boy is so black he's like a hole into hell," his grandmother said, swaddling the newborn. "He's got a hotline to the devil," she said. "Shave his head." And he stayed bald as he was black. Sure as you're born.

The boy is black where no one has ever been black: black palms and soles, black tongue—even the whites of his eyes are black. His healthy strong teeth are lined up like ebony soldiers in his mouth. The boy is so black his mother once lost him. The boy is so black, he was easy to find. At school, they call the boy over and use him to gauge the blackness of all the Black kids. Compared to the boy, no one is black.

One day a reporter steps out of his van, holds out a microphone, and asks the boy, "Can you see yourself in the dark?"

The boy looks into the camera's lens with his eyes as shiny and jet as marbles, and says, "Can you?"

When the interview airs, the boy's response causes a revolution in race relations. People wear black t-shirts with the words "Can you?" printed in black ink. Everyone wants to claim him. Some whites argue that the boy is too black to be Black; he must be white instead. Black people shake their heads in wonderment. It is understood that the blood that beats through this boy must be the purest blood: the very purest blood. Rumors begin that his blood heals ills—impotence, infertility, depression—everything but sickle-cell anemia. Dusky girls become the rage overnight, and new beauty products flood the marketplace: "darkens complexions invisibly" they advertise, "naturally brings out the deep tones of your hair."

People start using the word "black" to mean something total, absolute, transcendent. They analyze the boy's actions to understand what it means to be Black. Black, for instance, means waiting for the water to warm up before stepping into the shower. It's cracking your neck twice to the left and once to the right. It means being able to predict the trajectories of people moving through public space, their velocity and vector, and the safest distance between.

•

At some point, scientists notice the barest cooling of the surface of the earth, a slight dimming of the sun. After years of sifting through data, they traced the dimming to the exact date of the boy's birth. And so, the boy's fame is redoubled; he's lauded as a savior in this, our secular age; absorbing radiation to pardon us all, black and white, from the dangers of global warming, the sins of our fathers. Sure as you're born. Sure as you are.

The boy, now a man, shrugs his shoulders, enters some more numbers into his spreadsheet, and glows, just glows, in the heart of our country.

M.K. Foster

Because You Said *I Told You We Have Rock Rivers, But No Water*

and sent a photo—: the smooth stones arranged to form a dark vein

across the marbled gravel of your Arizona yard, a wire-limbed cactus,
an unsteadied, unstained rock retaining wall, all your mother's painted

metal animals, and the side of your house, bare and waiting, where inside
you and your father break your hungers together, share your silences, moving

together in and out of the bleached sound of a radio tuning in and out on
a lost satellite signal, heavy and unmoved as the sheetrock walls between

your bodies, as the hard-dry hollows you pass into and out of, stepping
around one another without speaking, wanting without saying what daughters

and fathers want to say in such spaces, all nerve, all glass, *I can't lose you like this*
and *I can't let you see me like this*, heavy as your sleep thick with dreams of lemons,

lemon trees, tossing and catching them in sleep that you share without
sharing and wake from alone in the night, the desert air bending, pouring though

the dented window screen, running through the center of you still empty clear
as an untouched glass of water on the bedside table in morning, dark and exact

as the scorpions you and your father catch together, their slick shells
glittering in starlight, broken black glass across the raw earth—: I remembered

how you turned away the winter I said *my father is a time bomb*, remembered your face
shrouded in shadow and cigarette smoke, your hands exposed, glowing red-cold,

ribboned with white cloud. Holding the photo, I remembered thinking how
the way you held your fist against your mouth told me in return *all fathers are.*

Clifton Gachagua

Cars

I dismember grasshoppers.
eat their frosty limbs,
hop over the carcasses of cars.
Yes, I need to migrate,
spread this plague, complete the
latitudes they have mapped on my vessels.
Collages of organs:
lying on the grass, I watch myself on Mars.

Carmen Giménez Smith

Radicalization

An agitator holds her sign up asking do you feel equal,
so you and your sisters deride her
because she's so public about injustice, so
second-wave. Your sisters gather around

her with scorn and sully her earnest nature. It's
thanks but no thanks. I can vote,
walk into the pharmacy for my Plan B, and wear
a chain wallet. One sister throws an apple

into the melee and the unfazed agitator bites it.
Her straight block-teeth break
the fruit apart which shocks your
sisters, but when they've abandoned their mockery

for the lure of a choice bazaar—earrings, Ugg boots,
removable tramp stamps,
a Sex and the City marathon—you're hot for
the agitator. The crowd clears and you kiss

her sweaty neck and use her agitating sign as a bed.
You scrawl her agitating words
onto your belly and stand naked against
her muscle memory. Not just the cause,

the impulse, the result, but the buzz
of lack. You'd like to consume it right
out of her, that humming electric
dissatisfaction. Then you'd like to put it

out of your body in the form
of a Louise Bourgeois sculpture, milky,
blobbing, love the star-fuckery
of doing it with her and to her, then

the sticky pulling apart,
the eternal production
of polyurethane eggs
wrapped in yarn.

from Post-Identity

an L city red silt-oil church massacre Go-Pro gunneries
poised missiles camps of refuge wounds from striking
innocent bystanders political kidnapper las mujeres de wherever
brown black corrective segregation the fudged numbers of food
supply water as currency meltdown sadism as foreign policy
SB1070 xenopublican prayer circle shootout martial idiom
infrastructure dismantling bacterial assassination boy-dictators
common rapacious industry vaccination discord fracking
separatists disability pain vendor indifferent law measures
for the preservation of strict class hierarchies too much goes
into history and becomes a series of wounds into the gauzy window
history as steamroller but it's also the refugee's lost luggage
sometimes you have more than you need, we are bound to
overlap yet you helm the vessel into the drip of our excess
sicario soccer the death of print means they own it all
more heartless colonialist in the extremist congress just want
my holes stopped up my mothers deported the disillusionment
of progress boomer red threat nostalgia ambivalence

Graça Graúna

Manifesto – I

...fragmento que sou
da fúria no choque cultural,
aqui, manifesto o meu receio
de não conhecer mais de perto
o que ainda resta
do cheiro do mato
da água
do fogo
da terra e do ar
Torno a dizer:
manifesto o meu receio
de não conhecer mais de perto
o cheiro da minha aldeia
onde ainda cunhantã
aprendi a ler a terra
sangrando por dentro.

Manifesto 1

…I am splintered
in the fury of cultural shock,
here, I manifest my fear
of not knowing more closely
what still remains
of jungle smell
of water of fire
of land of air

I say again:
I manifest my
fear of not knowing
more closely the smell
of my village
where when I was still
young I learned to read
the land bleeding inside.

Translated from the Portuguese via Spanish as an intermediary by Carolann Caviglia Madden

Caos climático

É temerário descartar
a memória das Águas
o grito da Terra
o chamado do Fogo
o clamor do Ar.

As folhas secas rangem sob os nossos pés.
Na ressonância o elo da nossa dor
em meio ao caos
a pavorosa imagem
de que somos capazes de expor
a nossa ganância
até não mais ouvir
nem mais chorar
nem meditar,
nem cantar...
só ganância, mais nada.

É temerário descartar
a memória das Águas
o grito da Terra
o chamado do Fogo
o clamor do Ar.

Climate Chaos

It is reckless to dismiss
water memory
the earth's keening
the call of fire
clamoring of air.

Dry leaves grind under our feet
in an echo of our grieving
amid the chaos of this
horrific image: our greed
displayed until we
are no longer
able to listen
or to mourn
or to meditate
or sing…
greed alone, nothing more.

It is reckless
to dismiss water
memory the earth's
keening the call
of fire clamoring
of air.

Translated from the Portuguese via Spanish as an intermediary by Carolann Caviglia Madden

FRANCINE J. HARRIS

sift

                                                            i am not all water
nor does the cue ball sink me
nor the cowboy rope me nor the monk
sit through me.

i am a thousand faces at
the bottom of the bottom's gravel. the
sea sharpened stones that clink and
soundless shift
make one.

and
i am not all river
not the sand on the tongue's first someone
or even a falling star.

i am all tooth and nail breaks
that bitter underwater
and a million years of sea-smash
dirt in your eye to dig out.

i am not all nigger:
a black hole crooning in the night
a country song in a deep jukebox
chewed down and rumbling.

so who decides
who belongs here,
which tooth should have been kicked out when.
which hole ought to be filled, this
is what i think:

every city has a country bar.
i am not always so tough when i walk in.

what is rain to the desert
is just another full mouth in some place like portland.

and i wonder if there are niggers here in oregon.
black-out dolls, wet and papery
their mouths full of chalk.

and some of you
don't go here either
looking for ground to settle
or a place to sit that isn't soggy and cold. same here.
everything grows damp, eventually.
anything can fall in.

i can put on a bad face, understand.
i can gunload and prostrate. could swallow you whole in any town.
i could keep from throwing the beer bottle, too.
keep from tearing up the green with my teeth.

but can i keep from being silt
from slipping wherever i go

and is everything something to rot
for our eyes to wriggle out of.

but, i am not all guilty.
nor can i be all sea.
this is just
a bone song. one we can both whistle along the skin to
in a skulk drag, down

through the rift.

Bob Hicok

Speaking American

When he learned I'm a poet he asked if I knew
this other poet. We don't all know each other,
I told him as he informed me she likes cheese
similes. Love is like cheese, time is like cheese,
cheese is surprisingly like cheese. Then I said
I know this poet and he went, see. "He went, see"
means he said see, see, but you know that
if you're American and alive. I explained
that "I know this poet" means "I know her work,"
when he was like, work? "When he was like"
is like "he went," which is past tense of "he goes,"
in case you're from another country and confused
by our lack of roundabouts. But poetry isn't work,
he said, unless you're talking about reading it.
But I'm not talking about reading it, I went,
in a moment that was the future past of everything
I'd do from then on. Such as snag the last
of the hyacinth cookies and step onto the veranda
to be awed by stars. Where I went, it's hard work,
to be awed by stars: they're just little lights
about which we learn a song as children.
And he was like, but I do wonder what they are,
as both of us lifted our heads like birds
waiting for our mother to throw up in our mouths.
When I shared the image, he was like, gross,
but then he went, you're right, that's what we do,
we expect the sky to feed us. This led
to a long discussion about yearning
in which the word yearning never appeared,
in which he went and I went and he was like
and I was like and the stars
kept doing what the song says they do,
because "burn your hydrogen burn your hydrogen
little star" doesn't fit the diatonic harmony
that pivots on an opposition between tonic and dominant
in a tune derived from "Ah, vous dirai-je, Maman."
Then a woman came out wearing a red dress

the size of a whisper, lit a smoke
and the smoke's smoke acted all floaty
and sexy and better than us, and she was like,
want one, and we were like, yes.

Lizz Huerta

milking

because my grandfather seeded as many women
as fields, these dark half-uncles roping and whistling

in the pasture are strangers with my father's face, their eyes
shaped the same for squinting, hands fat with muscle.

they show me how to pull the rope taut around
the beast's horns, ignore the bellows and heave.

squatting on a wooden box Payín with the silver teeth
talks me through the milking, long unused to intimacy

my hands shake on the teats. I press my face against
her warmth while in the pen her baby cries with hunger.

when the milk threatens to spill Payín pours, hands me
a bottle and tells me to feed Benito, a red calf born six days ago.

his mom's udder is filled only with pus and blood, they say
she is no good for breeding, when Lent is over she will

be sent to slaughter. I'll be home by then, far away from
this rocky place of the cross where my father was born.

when Benito finishes his bottle, I give him three fingers to
suck, his tongue as long as my hand, something in me leaps

at the unfamiliar heat of a soft hungry mouth, new mammal eyes.
at the other side of the pen Payín and another uncle force long

hollow needles into the bad teats, trying to drain the infection.
the cow rolls her eyes towards me and moans, long and low.

there isn't anything that can be done but wait and see if her body
swings back to what she was made for. when she is drained

I release Benito, he runs to his mama, he butts his head against her,
bleating, he sucks and sucks but she is dry.

on the ride back to the ranch I sit in the back of the truck
with the milk, my uncles telling me how like my grandfather I am,

the type of person who prefers sky and field to walls, I agree
though if I lived here I would have long ago been sent to slaughter.

Ishion Hutchinson

A Surveyor's Journal
for Wilson Harris

I took my name from the aftersky
of a Mesopotamian flood,
birdless as if culture had shed its wings
into a ground vulture on the plain.
Beneath the astral plane, a war-ripped sail,
rigged to its mast, a lantern and a girl,
who swayed and stared
off where the waves raced backwards.
I begged her in signs. She jumped
overboard, arms sieving seaweed, eyes netting home.

Dear Ivy, you live in my veins.
Spurned flesh, I couldn't bridle
the weathervane's shift; it turned and turned
into a landfall, and I, panting panther,
sleek carnivore of the horse-powered limbs,
ran from a reign of terror.
All my despairs in green rain, on leaves;
I prayed to the mantis, head wrapped
in white, reading the "Song of God"
over a bowl of beef. Afterwards,
I hemmed into my skin this hymn:

O lemming souls of the mass migration that ended in drowing
O embroidered heart and marigold wrists that brushed the copper-brown field
O cargoes that left the dengue jungles and ended on the yellow fever shores
O compass points that needled the new to the old, stitching meridians into one tense
O reflecting telescope that spied the endangered specimens

Clashing head-brass, the vertical man vs the horizontal man,
those who lost their surnames
to the sea's ledger, beached up on the strange coast,
waiting for the Star Liner
to the cross that imagined Mesopotamian water,
the ship's bulwarks in sleep,
weighed down a spirit-bird,
my calm, to never flounder,
to walk holy and light on this land.

Lauren Jensen-Deegan

Only You, My Husband as Smokey the Bear

I have lost all hope on keeping
the bathroom sink clean of fur. But then
I think of how lonely it is to be clean.
The way I was before you were
is a federally funded phrase that anyone
in a relationship can use so many words
blahblahblah to say just one: *love* or something
of the Two Bulls Fire still burning
but contained. Look how the wind lassos
the smoke through the pines. The way water falls
from helicopters as if the clouds listened
and filled with the fury that we prayed for
in the only language we know: to beg.
You hang your ranger hat on the elk shed
by the door. Suspend your blue suspenders
like a life long pledge over the back of a chair,
rub the darkness around your eyes. Paw
open to my hand then the button on my jeans.
So desperately we long for thumbs.

The Slow Race

Both men and women
              congregated
on their bikes
      and there was no order
                                  to this: everyone
just received a number
            and idled in a pool
                    of leather and chrome
waiting for their time to ride,
                        which arrived
      without a gunshot
      without a checkered flag thrown.

Imagine every contest beginning
                      with a grey mustache
          yelling "go." How during birth
  a young man
            would stand along
the soft/smooth side-
                lines of a woman's legs
and cheer, " Slow Down"
                        and years later
      in an empty house—

no super heroes spread across the floor
no cereal bowls with colored milk
no shoes piled by the door—

      my mother would run
her fingers through my father's
                    thinning hair
      and whisper,

"It happened so fast."

Not here, though.

Not there, either,
              at the Slow Race

where the experienced riders
                with decorated vests
of skulls and fringe
                        avoided the quick-
straight path and muscled
        their thousand pound cruisers
                            in a zigzag
along the dust course
                watered by a hose until
late afternoon
                  when the contest was over.

    no one moved because
    no one knew it had ended and
    no one knew who had won:

        it all happens that slow.

So gradual
                that some time later—
could have been hours,
            could have been years—
when the grey mustache
            stepped to the mike
and announced #27 the winner
                it was if there wasn't
                          a race at all.
    Just my brother and I,
men & women, doctors & thugs,
              Christians & dealers,
strangers mostly, together
on bikes
        who late in the night danced
to a cover band,
              took off our shirts,
      and even later,
                    revved engines
to honor all sons and daughters
still overseas

Amaud Jamaul Johnson

Pigmeat

Come to this common fallow of bone,
This body, hulking—this billowing robe.

Midday & the moonlight across my face.
Come: these hands, this beat, the broad

Hiccup, a smile. Here, when all the heat
Has been washed & wrung clean from the body

When the men begin to open their leather cases
& hold their monocles a little closer to my heart

& the parable of the homegrown &
The parable of the artificial Negro

Will be told. Here, with the sweet broadax
Of history, the thunderous applause.

Here comes the first crystal stair.
Here, come Hell or high-water; Hell

Or some falter. All the ease in legalese.
Here comes my tautology—

A blackness of a blackness of a blackness.
My monochromatic rainbow,

Articulate as a single finger haloing the moon.
A generation, spun-out or spooling & I'm dancing.

Here. Step Stutter-step, hush. I come.
Here comes the judge. Here comes the judge.

Claire Kageyama-Ramakrishnan

Terzanelle: Manzanar Riot

This is a poem with missing details,
of ground gouging each barrack's windowpane,
sand crystals falling with powder and shale,

where silence and shame make adults insane.
This is about a midnight of searchlights,
of ground gouging each barrack's windowpane,

of syrup on rice and a cook's big fight.
This is the night of Manzanar's riot.
This is about a midnight of searchlights,

a swift moon and a voice shouting, Quiet!
where the revolving searchlight is the moon.
This is the night of Manzanar's riot,

windstorm of people, rifle powder fumes,
children wiping their eyes clean of debris,
where the revolving searchlight is the moon,

and children line still to use the latrines.
This is a poem with missing details,
children wiping their eyes clean of debris—
sand crystals falling with powder and shale.

Ilya Kaminsky

We Lived Happily During the War

And when they bombed other people's houses, we

protested
but not enough, we opposed them but not

enough. I was
in my bed, around my bed America

was falling: invisible house by invisible house by invisible house.

I took a chair outside and watched the sun.

In the sixth month
of a disastrous reign in the house of money

in the street of money in the city of money in the country of money, our great country of money, we (forgive us)

lived happily during the war.

Joan Naviyuk Kane

the claim of the cliff above me
(or, ancient and brutal)

I went for relief of the mind, to move
into currents of worry. I did not
know what the body held.

I thought I would turn through
broken ice and disappear
these features of apprehension,

of influence. If only I could betray
the brute matter. If only the seas
had not erased the facture,

ladder, the easy reach.
Instead we sank into soft snow,
four women ascending together

the deep furrow worn by water
returning to water: Ayagaduk,
Uyuguluk, Yaayuk, Naviyuk.

I was startled, at once aware
that the far road had fractured,
done under by the fault

we fought to bury. Land rises
beyond three strong currents.
The boat that bears us rises

in them. With invisible stars
we share blood. Those seas,
increased, might scour and reflect—

those seas, increased, rephrase us.

an other lethe

The drag hook of the mind asthenic
catches yet on green not so gone
though scrolled in absent a horizon
banked with clouds turning forth,

driven by wind. Let us set nostalgia
in a harness. A pathogen is drawn
upstream from metal culvert buckled
in sweet brook water underroad again.

Let us see dust risen into light, subtracted
into rain. Our spring runs dry beneath
snow on a land now arid, now seam
of admonition: do not solve, adapt.

Katherine Larson

Love at Thirty-Two Degrees

I

Today I dissected a squid,
the late acacia tossing its pollen
across the black of the lab bench.
In a few months the maples
will be bleeding. That was the thing:
there was no blood
only textures of gills creased like satin,
suction cups as planets in rows. *Be careful
not to cut your finger*, he says. But I'm thinking
of fingertips on my lover's neck
last June. Amazing, hearts.
This branchial heart. After class,
I stole one from the formaldehyde
and watched it bloom in my bathroom sink
between cubes of ice.

II

Last night I threw my lab coat in the fire
and drove all night through the Arizona desert
with a thermos full of silver tequila.

It was the last of what we bought
on our way back from Guadalajara—
desert wind in the mouth, your mother's
beat-up Honda, agaves
twisting up from the soil
like the limbs of cephalopods.

Outside of Tucson, saguaros so lovely
considering the cold, and the fact that you
weren't there to warm me.
Suddenly drunk I was shouting that I wanted to see the stars
as my ancestors used to see them—

to see the godawful blue as Aurvandil's frostbitten toe.

III

Then, there is the astronomer's wife
ascending stairs to her bed.

The astronomer gazes out,
one eye at a time,

to a sky that expands
even as it falls apart

like a paper boat dissolving in bilge.
Furious, fuming stars.

When his migraine builds and
lodges its dark anchor behind

the eyes, he fastens the wooden buttons
of his jacket, and walks

outside with a flashlight
to keep company with the barn owl

who stares back at him with eyes
that are no greater or less than

a spiral galaxy.
The snow outside

is white and quiet
as a woman's slip

against cracked floorboards.
So he walks to the house

inflamed by moonlight, and slips
into the bed with his wife

her hair and arms all
in disarray

like fish confused by waves.

                IV

Science—

beyond pheromones, hormones, aesthetics of bone,
every time I make love for love's sake alone,

I betray you.

Mariama J. Lockington

prunus persica

>to one moment

>be a clingstone

>flesh sticking to the pit

>perfect for canning

>the next

>a freestone

>a slice severed neatly

>from the hard center

>the girl dreamt

>pink blossoms

>felt a ripening

>in her chest

>a lovely brown rot

>in her bones

TARIQ LUTHUN

New Rule
*reference: dark like dirt but not like dirt

        if when

        you are going to kill

        a person, you must first

        ^[black/brown]*   learn our names,

look us   in the eyes   & say them aloud.

                                        no more

                                        learning

our names after

                                        we're dead.

Thomas Lux

Lump of Sugar on an Anthill

The dumb ants hack and gnaw it off grain by grain
and haul it down to the chamber
where they keep such things
to feed their queen and young. The smart ants
dig another entrance, wait for rain.
Which melts the sugar,
and through viaducts they direct it
to their nurseries, the old ants' home, the unantennaed ward,
and so on—the good little engineering ants!
The dumb ants have to eat their sugar dry.
Put your ear to a dumb ant's anthill's hole—mandibles on
sandpaper is what you'll hear.
The dumb ants pray it doesn't rain before
they've done their task,
or else they will drown—in sweetness,
but drown, nonetheless.

Travis Macdonald

Maine

Norway maple, common yarrow, sneezewort yarrow, common horse chestnut, colonial bentgrass, redtop, creeping bentgrass, redroot pigweed, common ragweed, stinking chamomile, sweet vernalgrass, great burdock, common burdock, tall oatgrass, mugwort, halberdleaf orach, yellow rocket, Japanese barberry, common barberry, hoary alyssum, Indian mustard, black mustard, birdsrape mustard, smooth brome, rye brome, hedge bindweed, creeping bellflower, shepherd's-purse, common caraway, oriental bittersweet, bittersweets, brown knapweed, black knapweed, common mouse-ear chickweed, big chickweed, greater celandine, lambsquarters, chicory, Canada thistle, bull thistle, field bindweed, orchardgrass, February daphne, Queen Anne's lace, maiden pink, smooth crabgrass, large crabgrass, barnyardgrass, Russian olive, quackgrass, helleborine, wallflower mustard, cypress spurge, buckwheat, wild buckwheat, Japanese knotweed, hard fescue, meadow fescue, sheep fescue, queen-of-the-meadow, glossy buckthorn, common hempnettle, hairy galinsoga, smooth bedstraw, yellow bedstraw, herb-robert, ground ivy, American mannagrass, low cudweed, tawny daylily, dames rocket, orange hawkweed, meadow hawkweed, mouseear hawkweed, kingdevil hawkweed, live-forever stonecrop, witch's moneybags, common St. Johnswort, Himalayan balsam, elecampane, European sticktight, fall hawkbit, motherwort, field pepperweed, oxeye daisy, yellow toadflax, common flax, perennial ryegrass, Morrow's honeysuckle, bush honeysuckles, Tatarian honeysuckle, showy fly honeysuckle, birdsfoot trefoil, creeping Jenney, garden loosestrife, purple loosestrife, paradise apple, musk mallow, common mallow, pineapple-weed, black medic, yellow sweetclover, peppermint, true forget-me-not, catnip, red bartsia, wild-proso millet, wild parsnip, ladysthumb, reed canarygrass, timothy, European common reed, Norway spruce, buckhorn plantain, broadleaf plantain, annual bluegrass, Canada bluegrass, prostrate knotweed, marshpepper smartweed, common purslane, silvery cinquefoil, sulfur cinquefoil, tall buttercup, bulbous buttercup, creeping buttercup, wild radish, European buckthorn, cultivated currant, bristly locust, yellow fieldcress, cinnamon rose, sweetbriar rose, multiflora rose, Seaside rose, red sorrel, curly dock, longleaf dock, broadleaf dock, birdseye pearlwort, white willow, crack willow, laurel willow, purpleosier willow, Russian thistle, bouncing-bet, woodland groundsel, common groundsel, foxtail millet, yellow foxtail, bristlegrass, green foxtail, green bristlegrass, meadow campion, white campion, bladder campion, nightflowering catchfly, wild mustard, tumble mustard, hedge mustard, bittersweet nightshade, black nightshade, perennial sowthistle, field sowthistle, spiny sowthistle, annual sowthistle, false spiraea, European mountain-ash, corn spurry, red sandspurry, little starwort, common chickweed, claspleaf twistedstalk, common lilac, common tansy, rock dandelion, field pennycress, meadow salsify, rabbitfoot clover, hop clover, large hop clover, alsike clover, red clover, white clover, coltsfoot, common valerian, moth mullein, common mullein, corn speedwell, common speedwell, thymeleaf speedwell, European cranberrybush, European highbush cranberry, bird vetch, common vetch, sparrow vetch

Oklahoma

velvetleaf, common yarrow, jointed goatgrass, tree-of-heaven, mimosa, prostrate pigweed, redroot pigweed, common ragweed, annual ragweed, stinking chamomile, thymeleaf sandwort, yellow bluestem, field brome, rescuegrass, bald brome, rye brome, cheatgrass, paper-mulberry, corn gromwell, hedge bindweed, smallseed falseflax, shepherd's-purse, balloonvine, musk thistle, bittersweets, cornflower, common mouse-ear chickweed, big chickweed, sticky chickweed, lambsquarters, sweet autumn virginsbower, Asiatic dayflower, poison-hemlock, field bindweed, bermudagrass, jimsonweed, Queen Anne's lace, wild carrot, flixweed, Deptford pink, large crabgrass, mexicantea, clammy goosefoot, junglerice, barnyardgrass, Russian olive, goosegrass, stinkgrass, weeping lovegrass, redstem filaree, bushy wallflower, toothed spurge, wild buckwheat, tall fescue, Italian ryegrass, meadow fescue, common St. Johnswort, ivyleaf morningglory, tall morningglory, Mexican fireweed, Kummerowia, Korean lespedeza, common lespedeza, prickly lettuce, henbit, purple deadnettle, shrubby lespedeza, sericea lespedeza, oxeye daisy, Chinese privet, privet, yellow toadflax, perennial ryegrass, Japanese honeysuckle, bush honeysuckles, common mallow, white horehound, black medic, alfalfa, yellow sweetclover, spearmint, white mulberry, parrotfeather, Eurasian water-milfoil, watercress, catnip, ragweed, parthenium, dallisgrass, perilla mint, ladysthumb, European common reed, buckhorn plantain, annual bluegrass, black bindweed, marshpepper smarweed, rabbitfoot polypogon, common purslane, sulfur cinquefoil, kudzu, bristly locust, multiflora rose, red sorrel, curly dock, Russian-thistle, bouncingbet, yellow foxtail, bristlegrass, green foxtail, green bristlegrass, field madder, wild mustard, tumble mustard, hedge mustard, spiny sowthistle, johnsongrass, common chickweed, fivestamen tamarisk, smallflower tamarisk, saltcedar, tamarisk, rock dandelion, field pennycress, spreading hedgeparsley, Japanese hedge-parsley, western salsify, puncturevine, large hop clover, small hop clover, red clover, white clover, Siberian elm, moth mullein, common mullein, corn speedwell, common vetch, hairy vetch

David Maduli

St. Mary's Park Ghazal

fourth generation great-grandchildren of this house
dishes break but bedrock solid when earth quakes this house
always red front stairs the tongue of this house
great-lola approaches one hundred in this house
year of my birth the family moved to this house
outer mission warm as ilocos at this house
skateboard five minutes to bart from this house
mah jong tiles click clack in this house
lolo's ghost patrols wood floors of this house
slide on socks kitchen to bay window in this house
jump down back stairs to the garage of this house
mom lay cold on the living room floor in this house
unwrapped presents birthday cakes in this house
alemany flea market uphill to this house
who will live here when lola's gone from this house?
only one place called home, this house
this city this family this blood, this house

Nick Makoha

Prayers for Exiled Poets

> *Were you to ask me where I've been...*
> *I would have to tell how dirt mottles the rocks,*
> *how the river, running, runs out of itself...*
> —Pablo Neruda
> *from* "There's No Forgetting (Sonata)"
> translated by Forrest Gander

Prayers no longer hold up these walls in my absence.
My own country rebukes me. I hold the world on my back.

Look for me in translation. In my own language you will go unanswered.
My Ugandan passports are a quiet place of ruin.

Where I come from, money is water slipping through their hands.
They eat what falls from the trees and turns the flesh to gin.

I am of the same fruit and close to extinction.
My only root is my father's name. Both of us removed from the soil.

In recent times, despite my deeds, you let me stay
no longer in bondage between earth and sky. No longer

do I hide in my own shadow. No longer waiting to stop waiting.
This rock becomes a sanctuary from which I can repair the ruins.

You have given me back my eyes.

Sally Wen Mao

Provenance: A Vivisection

> *[The Bodies exhibition] is a redemocratization. The human body is the last remaining nature in a man-made environment.*
> —Gunther von Hagens

    I.

You, you are a factory
of muscle. You, you are an empire
of polymer. I recognize myself

in your face, your posture, your severed
epiglottis. Take it off. Take it all off
for us to see: first the clothes,

then the epidermis, then your mouth,
your country, your context. Provenance:
a chronology of ownership—

all tautology, for none of our emissaries
have uncovered the tampered body's
histories. The prophet calculates

the profits. Exhibit A: Hottentot Venus.
Pregnant woman from village X,
reclining nude in lit interior. Excision—

watch the womb peeled back,
see what milkless plastic the baby
suckles, how he crows against the vernix

of his mother's plastic gluetrap. Baby,
do you dream of trapezes? Baby, do
you choke on the inchoate cloud?

    II.

Gunther von Hagens was born in Poland,
    January 1945. That season, snow
shuddered everywhere and ashes too descended
from crematoriums onto frozen glades.

Mao

The Turkish poet Nazim Hikmet wrote
to his wife from prison: *even at the dump*
          our atoms will fall side by side.

Tired fires cleaved through cities, rivers
choked on human glands. Hemophilia wracked
von Hagens' childhood: blood scissored out
at every gust. Decades later, he invented
plastination to tame the rogue artery.
He becomes Doctor, curator of skulls,
inventor of perfect preservation:
it takes three years to plastinate an elephant.
Two for a horse, just one for a man.

    III.

You, you are my clout, menagerie.
When I imagine your bedroom
positions, you will enact my fantasies.

In my dreams, I ask you to stop licking
your pelt, whip you like an elder god.
Your fats, sternums, orifices

will educate us, provide the jolt
for a Sunday afternoon. Soil
yourself and I'll be the one to wipe you,

I'll be the one to flense your skin.
Exhibit B: Chang and Eng.
Exhibit C: Kamala and Amala.

Exhibit D: Ota Benga, St. Louis
World Fair, 1904. It's a simple
exchange. We will pay for you.

Your hanging organs—our garden.
Gelatins astound us, fill us with relief

for what we have: golden hearts

that rouge the very air around.
Lungs that breathe. Gills that sing.
We are an abattoir of gratitude.

    IV.

This is a fatty market. It blooms a corpulent
flower. Body suppliers. Rafflesia. Rapeseed. Boom,

boom, drones the Dalian corpse plant. Production
line: technicians dehydrate faces, bones, cartilage,

soak the cadavers in pink effluvia.
Autopsy hour—watch the fatty tissues sap,

seep, curdle. Watch the sticky plastic pump
into their ribs, ravish them. Kiss the cadaver

with a scalpel. Knives pare their eyes. Bad pears:
cores swarm with gnats, millipedes, wormseeds.

Insects coil over their golden flesh. Their
mouths are blood diamonds. Rumor has it,

the world is gorging on Chinese secrets.
Cover this wound before the flies find it.

    V.

Sir, I look at you through your vitreous blue
eyes, and your shorn life passes through me
in one thrush. Boy who flunked his college

entrance exams. Man who ate abalone
from the can. How were you punished?
With bullwhips and jellyfish stings?

Mao

You died not long ago: I can tell by the way
your ligaments curl. Have you traveled
as far in your life as you've toured

posthumously, torqued in a prison
of cryogenic light? Amsterdam. Paris.
New York: what does it mean, anyway—

the provenance of a corpse? Who may possess
the body—spirit, demon, man, enter-
prise? You cannot exorcise the black

market from the body, though I want to smash
that slipshod glass, obliterate the price
on your head. I want to wreck the paraffin

that suspends your dancing spine in the air.
I scratch the cage, wipe your name
in pellucid bones. When they kick me

out, I search for you in my father's face
and find you in my son's. Pittsburgh's
highways soliloquize your anonymity,

your face on the billboard a marvel.
You gaze at my city with your pupils
sealed. Wherever I go now, you follow.

Lately, my neck grows inward, a headless
stump. Lately, the cumulonimbus tears
open the aspens. The sun, too, has a blade.

    VI.

Thief of my skin, you can arrange my bones so I fly,

a raptor—you can cure my meat, summon the flies
in summer. My body is my crypt, your masterpiece.
Turkey vultures scare the stratosphere
searching for carrion, follow the scent in my limbs,
its feral suet. My name does not end in fury.
I'd rather you blow my alien bits into a black hole
than keep me here, intact and jaundiced. So please,
I ask: incinerate me. Let the sky be my open grave.

Adrian Matejka

Map to the Stars

A Schwinn-ride away: Eagledale Plaza. Shopping strip
of busted walkways, crooked parking spaces nicked
like the lines on the sides of somebody's mom-barbered
head. Anchored by the Piccadilly disco, where a shootout
was guaranteed every weekend, those gun claps: coughing
stars shot from sideways guns shiny enough to light the way
for anyone willing to keep a head up long enough to see.
Not me. I bought the Star Map Shirt for 15¢ at the Value
Village next to the Piccadilly during the daytime. The shirt
was polyester with flyaway collars, outlined in the forgotten
astronomies of disco. The shirt's washed-out points of light:
arranged in horse & hero shapes & I rocked it in places
neither horse nor hero hung out. Polyester is made from
polyethylene & catches fire easily like wings near a thrift store
sun. Polyethylene, used in shampoo bottles, gun cases,
& those grocery sacks skidding like upended stars across
the parking lot. There are more kinds of stars in this universe
than salt granules on drive-thru fries. Too many stars,
lessening & swelling with each pedal pump away from
the Value Village as the electric billboard above flashes first
one DUI attorney, then another who speaks Spanish so the sky
above is constantly chattering, like the biggest disco ball ever.

EPMD Feat. Emily Dickinson

I love poetry slipping the spindles of happenstance,
its em dashery like the closed eye of a winking man
used for a record needle. I love when the laces

of my suede kicks undo like the best laid plans. & when
I crouch to tie those boys up, I love savoring the shy
glory of my girl's skirted knee. Her stitched hem

branching like the feathered stems in a blue boa
she would never wear. The first feather in that garish
elegance: America, home of lovers & EPMD breaking

car speakers like high school curfews since 1988
someplace where I loved summer, the dash from one
hoop to the other, a stray kitten in the bleachers chewing

a moth before we fed him a hamburger & somebody's
Business as Usual cassette untangling like laughs.

Sounds of Earth

Voyager's Golden Records
were spinning someplace

between Uranus & Neptune
      the night I pedaled

      my new 10-speed
along Georgetown Road's

unfinished edge & the driver
      of a Datsun necked out

of his passenger window yelling
      Off the road, nigger.

His mouth was uncollected
& full of open teeth—

right there, screaming
in my face like our ball coach

during line laps hollering
      about Bobby Knight.

& then I was in a ditch—

      front wheel bent in half,
as useless as half a surprise.

After that, more constellations
connecting the dots. No more

      crickets or Miles Davis
valving the Walkman

or quick soda trips to the VP.

Sitting there, in the cricketed
   grass of the ditch I heard

all the same sounds
etched in copper

   & plated in gold
for the long ride out
   into a universe

spinning so unrelentingly

   I kept losing parts
of myself between inhales.

Erika Meitner

By Other Means

My body as terra nullias. My body as celestial. My body as dysfunctional. This water-damaged waiting room. This explicable flood of couples with expectant grins. The grim single-mother with hair past her waist and plastic Dollar Tree bag as purse. The girl in the hallway asking about my hair, diamond studs on either side of her lip pinning her smile. This exam table. This white sheet below my waist. This white sheet reeking of bleach.   Your wisecracking Resident. Your overly-friendly Resident. Your Resident making me anonymous.   Your Resident making me ashamed.   I will show you, Resident, the corner of Detroit where the houses love me, my sheen, since I am as cavernous, as broken-down. Where the houses don't talk back or ask how the procedure went. The vast   territory of my ovaries on screen,   their black holes,   their stellar mass. The whole solar system is bursting, splintering, flaring, and I am not. Planets spin   on their axes and   people are launched   into space.   I am   the territory   no one will inhabit. The borderlands of *motherland* and *not again.*   Want has no business here.

Jennifer Minniti-Shippey

Last Days of June

A whole sun-skinned nation
later and I am on my knees
in the trolley, the trolley south
bound, everything dark and rattling—
June in this country comes
jacarandad and sky-bruised—and me
wailing hallelujah quite
silently, good-bye brave ponies
grazing in the green wind, good-
bye thin socks abandoned
to the soft mercies of rain,
good-bye plastic peonies on the high
heels of happiness.
I am trying, just try
ing to love this, my life, again.

MICHAEL MLEKODAY

The History of the Black Market

started with the archaeologists.
When a new species of prehistoric beast

was discovered at a dig in North Dakota,
paleontologist Robert Frost went rogue—

first he stole a tusk and sold it to a local church.
The trick caught on like a spark

in a California wood. Soon all kinds of bones
were in circulation, and finally, whole skeletons.

Kanye copped a new Jesus piece
made of pure African pterodactyl.

Malcolm X started rocking Tyrannosaurus specs.
Make no bones about it, the eco-terrorists said:

*first they came for the dinosaur bones, and I
didn't speak out because I wasn't a dinosaur bone.*

The Marxists elbowed their way
into the conversation. They claimed

it was the agenda of Global Capital
to alienate the worker from her bones.

Global Capital laughed. An eco-critic
shot Robert Frost in the face.

As the cultural climate overheated—
or, some historians speculate, froze over

until the whole icy matter burned
whatever it touched—the feds

busted the black market, prompting the rise
of the bootleggers. Billy Collins

whipped together fake bones that crumbled
under scrutiny. Pusha T constructed the frame

of a venom-spitting dino by compressing
four-hundred pounds of cocaine

and shaving it into shape with a twenty dollar bill.
Some bootleggers started pawning off human bones

as the real thing, including some kids
from Philly who jacked Derrick Rose's knee.

There were street fights. There were gang wars.
Eventually, in what became known

as the Easter Rising, St. Scott La Rock re-appeared
in the Bronx to issue a sermon, calling for a stop

to the in-fighting, arguing that this was all a conspiracy,
that the war on bone-sellers was nothing more

than an excuse for the white male elite
to further entrench their power,

burying it deep in the earth, pretending
it had been there the whole time.

The History of the Lumberjack

Paul Bunyan was a hero to most,
but he never meant shit to Chuck D.

D argues that flannel was the name
of the first negro spiritual

and that Bunyan's appropriation
of the axe was an affront to the memory

of Nat Turner. Record executives claim
Babe the Blue Ox had better flow

than Flavor Flav, but he rejected
an invitation to join Public Enemy

on the grounds that they were from Long Island
and not actually members of the proletariat.

Marxist scholars dispute this, asserting
that the beef between the two camps

is a bourgeois conspiracy meant to drive
a wedge between lumberjacks and emcees,

the two vanguards of the revolution.
The history is muddied.

Still, backpackers say they know the truth:
in the 19th Century, they claim, before

the commercials made him one giant
ad campaign for the timber industry, Paul Bunyan

was known to his followers as MC Bonyenne.
His first mixtape, *The Papineau Rebellion*,

killed more Brits than a guerilla war.
Once, when Harriet Tubman

was helping runaways cross the border,
she found Bonyenne praying at the river.

She brought him down to Virginia
to meet Captain John Brown,

who introduced his name to Americans.
But Bonyenne and Bunyan

are two different people, or,
more accurately, Bunyan is a lie.

Babe the Blue Ox isn't real either,
but purists still believe in Flavor Flav.

Bonyenne never turned pop.
Some old-timers still say that,

every year on Bonyenne's birthday,
if you follow the North Star to the woods

where he is rumored to have been born,
wading along the banks of the river, you'll find

the widest stump you've ever seen. Circle
the tree-rings with your fingers and listen

closely: it's as if the whole wilderness
has been freestyling here forever.

Felix Mnthali

Neocolonialism

Above all, define standards
prescribe values
set limits; impose boundaries

and even if you have no satellites
in space
and no weapons of any value
you will rule the world

Whatever tune you sing
they will dance
whatever bilge you spill
they will lick
and you may well pick
and choose
their rare minerals
and their rich forests

They will come to you
in fear and trembling
for the game will be played
according to your rules
and therefore the game will be played
only when you can win

Above all,
prescribe values
and define standards
and then sit back
to allow the third world
to fall into your lap.

Carrie Moniz

Year Two of Your Seven-Year Sentence: Midnight Ride to Yuma

Do you face the road? Did you see the lights
    approaching for miles?

Visitation was over hours ago. Guards in grey
towers, have me in their sights.
But I've got what I came for,
    nameless, quiet.

•

Of the windows, no bigger than a brick,
which looks out from your cell? Which sees
a woman walking from walls, lost

as a blind man in dunes? God and trains
keep finding their way
into her words. *The cars are open to the canopy*

which is the open sky.

A woman walking from prison
sees a spectacle of legs
walking from prisons for centuries.

David Mura

Summers with the JACL

The picnic consisted of teriyaki, *tsukemono*,
and since some things were lost in translation,
rice balls. Three-legged races before the rain broke
and a raffle where I won a gallon of shoyu.

"*Nihonjin or hakujin?*" was a question I'd hear
but never knew exactly what it meant
though I hunted for the latter so many years
I wed one: a shiksa and a daughter of Rachel too.

George seemed a quicker moniker than Mas;
Mary outran Michiko. What kanji
you were born with didn't matter. Or years
in the desert, the mountains, the Arkansas swamp.

Years later I wrote my first poem about my *ojī-chan*
—whom I never called *ojī-chan*—in a room
where rain poured through the ceiling
in a metal bucket, not knowing that wasn't an end

but the beginning of so many lost worlds
as the leaking heavens still pour down
and shout to my mother and father
hopping to the finish line—*Go, go, go…*

ANGEL NAFIS

Gravity
    after Carrie Mae Weems's "The Kitchen Table Series"

I. THE STRAW

Can you throw this away Maybe you should hire more Black staff
Where are you really from You're not busy are you You look ethnic today
Where's the African American section Can you turn the music down
Fasterfasterfaster Let me see those eyes Beautiful If you were mine
I'd never let you leave the house It's like you went straight to Africa
to get this one Is that your hair I mean your real hair Blackass
Your gums are black You Black You stink You need a perm
I don't mean to be
racist

But
You're scarred over, I'm the one bleeding
You're just going to rip apart whatever I say
You've said sorry only two times
We tacitly agreed
Then dead me

II. THE CAMEL'S BACK

When you born on somebody else's river in a cursed boat it's all downhill from there. Ha. Just kidding. I'd tell you what I don't have time for but I don't have time. Catch up. Interrogate that. Boss. Halo. I juke the apocalypse. Fluff my feathers. Diamond my neck. Boom, like an 808. One in a million. I don't want no scrubs. You don't know my name. Everything I say is a spell. I'm twenty-five. I'm ninety. I'm ten. I'm a moonless charcoal. A sour lover. Hidden teeth beneath the velvet. I'm here and your eyes lucky. I'm here and your future lucky. Ha. God told me to tell you I'm pretty. Ha. My skin Midas-touch the buildings I walk by. Ha. Every day I'm alive the weather report say: Gold. I know. I know. I should leave y'all alone, salt earth like to stay salty. But here go the mirror, egging on my spirit. Why I can't go back. Or. The reasons it happened. Name like a carriage of fire. Baby, it's real. The white face peeking through the curtain. Mule and God. I'm blunted off my own stank. I'm Bad. I dig graves when I laugh.

Diana Khoi Nguyen

Self-Portrait with Strider Wolf

What can you tell a man at the margins?
    His bible bears his name.

What can you tell a man?
    You are one mind in the commune of one
    dropping his white robe for shredding.
    A womb-born creature that must fly
    as if frightened by its body.

Where did you go?
    With the woman in the elevator
    holding a cricket cage.

What did you collect?
    A beak peaking through a drum.
    Ossicles, old echoer. A stirrup is
    the smallest bone.

What did it feel like?
    Like this: / / ////   /   / / / / // // // / /// / /// / / / / // /
    / / / // // / / / / / / / /
    /// / / / / / / / / / // / / / / // / /

And you collected shadows?
    In the house my father tried to build.
    I'd grown up seeing America disarming others
    to protect itself.

A sort of guardianship?

> The goose has always been
> a goose. It has never been a man
> whose fathers lie like mountain-ruins
> within him.

Do they give you grief?

> Pain outlives its vehicle. Illness comes
> like a veil in the attic cordoning off tender
> of the mind.

Did you cure yourself?

> America now arming itself. My wounds
> spoke to me. They said:
> "Kneel down beside your brothers on the floor."

And?

> And bray.

from **Matrilineal: Life *Au Naturel***

Turns out the harmony of the world needed someone starving
White swan now gone, white shadow crossing that black pond, sidereal, blood on the egg bark, is not the body more light than not
Yield
I dreamed of four dogs performing a circus trick in my room—a fifth dog came into the room much smaller than the other dogs, bit all the other dogs to death
Insects running in and out of cracks in the ceiling plaster: from the corner of our eye, something we saw, imaging more of them, or less of them, like a mother when her children exhaust her
Houses can be ghosts, too, just like brothers
I must've been a young woman once
One day a sullen man shoved a woman toward the doorknob, but the man was a son, and the woman was his mother, and they lived as families do ever after
Actually, she protected me by ignoring me, my passion for milk, uncontrollable still
I played with myself just to arouse you
All good children covet their feed, so sabotage your crops accordingly
I praise the moon for suffering men but the Clark telescope shows it as pockmarked as any of us
Nothing is all

Nicole Parizeau

Bridgework

A sailor   **A soldier**

is a brick laid on its end,   is also a brick laid on its end

  V   C   its   V   but
                                                             E
  E   A   broad   R
                                                            T   only
  R   L   face   I
                                                            C   in
  T   L   ex-   A
                                                            L
  I   Y,   posed   L   pro-
                                                            Y,   file.

A basket weave
is pairs of sailors laid side by side,
capped with a shiner,
alternating with
pairs of sailors laid side by side,
atop a shiner.

                    (A shiner
                    is a brick laid on its

                n   a   r   r   o   w

              side, its broad face exposed.)

In brickwork

a quoin is a corner,
the angle of a wall or a bridge,
or a man,

in which case it might be called a quoin
of the realm
but not if it lives under bridges.

Establish a bond.

>The trick for bricks
>to be stable
>under a modest load is
>that they be laid in a bond.
>
>To preserve a certain bond, you lay
>a three-quarter bat at the quoin of the wall.
>This fact has no bearing on the appearance of the wall;
>to the spectator, the brick looks
>like any ordinary header.

>>**(A bat**
>>is a shard of brick good only
>>for cramming into spaces
>>too small for the real thing.)

In a Raking Monk Bond

the brickwork contains minor errors, some of which
have been silently corrected
with compensating irregularities in a course farther up.
The disposal of bricks in a Raking Monk
can be challenging.

Sometimes it's a replica.

The First Consideration of Ratio

is that the bed of a brick
is the mortar on which it is laid.

A perPEND is the vertical joint
between two bricks
and is usually,
but not always,
filled with mortar.

The coordinating principle is that
the total width of two bricks
plus
a perpend of mortar
is equal to the length of a single brick.

This is how bridges are built.

Construction and Behavior of Arch Bridges

Brick arches are strong and resistant to settlement
or undermining.
That is, they're strong in compression but
cave under tension.
Brick arch bridges are designed to be constantly under compression
as far as possible.

Masonry Design for Disproportionate Collapse

has evolved, but the implications are
not as far-reaching as you may have heard.

You must still prove that
the walls, columns, and beams can be
removed,
one at a time,
without causing collapse.

Exceptions:

Of course there's always the chance
of collapse
of an arch bridge
close to a fault line.

        Genetics

        Brick wicks moisture
        from the foundation or
        relays it from
        a wet patch of ground.
        The manifest result is called
        damp.

                The American Bond

                also goes by the name of
                the Common Bond.
                Ask anyone here
                about the American Bond
                and he'll tell you.

I commend to you this brick,

this soldier,
inserted into the quoin
of the pier in the arch of
the span above my head. This
brick—of all the bricks I know by
heart from waking daily together under
tension under the bridge—this brick is my rock,
and remembers me from my former days.
But more: its verticality comforts me.
The mortar that surrounds this
brick has bound my wits and
borne my load and guards
me softly against
collapse.

This, too, is bridgework.

Patrick Rosal

Delenda Undone

And so we've all been told to shutup (*Don't talk*, they say,
*too fast, too loud, or for too long. Don't take too much time
trying to tell the truth*). But this is my work,
to break out—in the presence of strangers—into laughter,
to watch small children, for example, fill with the lucky gust
a poem can ride into the near stillness of a room
and dance. For that, I am always, as now, grateful.

My father tells me, in his seminary days,
during the Japanese occupation,
most of the priests who ran that school were German.
The boys, then, were the speak only in Latin,
and would surely be slapped three Sundays back
if heard speaking the language of my father's country,
which is a beautiful country and a beautiful language,
and which has a curious word for being
so suddenly seized by affection, you clench
every muscle from your eyelids to your toes
for wanting to hold a loved one tight, to squeeze one
and kiss one so deep, you place yourself and your beloved
on the brink of physical harm. There's no word for this
in English, no word for those small provinces of silence
or for the kind of love that will trouble that silence
into music. My work is trying to find the very word
rippling in my body, which is a woman's body,
and mother's, and a man's body, my father's,
and nowhere to be found in the languages
that have conquered the lands of my ancestors.

On the outskirts of every empire, there are man-made
lakes large enough to receive with ease
one hundred villages' worth of bones tossed into them.
This is a fact: there are more than seven million Ilocanos
in the Phillippines, maybe a million in diaspora. All of us,
at one time or another, have been told to shutup, don't talk
too loud, too slow, or for too long, in Saudi
Arabia, in Madrid, in Tokyo, in Milan, on Bowery
near the foot of 1st Street. We've been told this. Some of us

have been famous liars, Ferdinand for example
(who married another liar, Imelda), and my grandfather,
kapitan of the barrio, who claimed to kick the shit
bare-fisted and single-handedly out of fourteen ruffians
in the small barangay of Santa Tomás. Actually,
he kicked the shit out of five—nine ran away. These are not
lies. This is the truth. I'm not wealthy. I can't buy
space and time on billboards or websites. The name I inherit
doesn't part columns in the city's Daily Journal.
My family comes from a long line of farmers.
My cousins scrub their chopping blocks with salt.
They shush the goats before they kill them.

CRAIG SANTOS PEREZ

America's Third Coming

Dredging and dredging in the widening harbor;
The whales are deafened by navy sonar;
Reefs fall apart; our island cannot hold;
Invasive species unleashed upon the shore,
The sewers flood Marine Corps Drive, everywhere
The day of liberation is crowned;
Politicians lack conviction, while businessmen
Arrive with predatory investments.

Securely, the America cuffs our hands;
Securely, the Third Coming will desecrate our lands.
No to the military buildup! We raise our voices
As sunburnt tourists take selfies;
We stare in fear: in the waves of the Pacific
A shape with eagle body and tip of the spear,
A gaze imperial and valiant as a shield,
Is moving its slow violence, while all around us
flock ghosts of extinct native birds.
The pivot has begun; but now we know
after a century of colonial sleep
we awaken from nightmare in a weapons cradle,
America's war beast, its feeding time come round again,
Carriers towards Guam to be berthed.

The American

One must have a mind of America
To disregard the wire and the barbs
Of military fences crusted with sand;

And have been American a long time
To behold our mouths jagged with English,
The hotels shining in the distant glint

Of the Territorial sun; and not to think
Of any misery in the choke of our voice,
In the unearthed mound of bones,

Which is the pain of our land
Full of maimed voices
Crashing against the eroded shore

For the American, who occupies the sand,
And, everything himself, claims
Everything that is not his until everything is.

Staci R. Schoenfeld

The Deconstruction of Dorothy Parker

Acids	are					
cramp	aren't	.				
drugs	cause	.				
Gas	give	;				
Guns	live	;				
Nooses	might	;	awful			
Razors	pain	;	damp	you		
Resumé	smells	;	lawful	you		
Rivers	stain	;	well	You	And	as

Matthew Shenoda

from *Tahrir Suite*, III: The Migration

To settle from one geography to another
Seemed to make no difference
Tekla was strange in a strange land
Chance was the culture he yearned
To resettle once and again was now a matter of taste
Nothing could be bound, it seemed
Everything tethered would soon vanish

Isis watched as the imprints on the footpath increased
Held by a small reflection of light
She caught her thoughts in midair
Broken only by her child's laughter
She wondered what she might remember
In a place where all she did was learn

When he woke that winter morning
He understood that heat could overcome cold
He walked the streets transfigured
Imagined the multiplicity of his face

The news came quick
Like a memory escaped from a dark hollow
The dead were mounting in number
Each a similar name

How swiftly they turned from present to past
Could not find a name for prudence
Rested on a broken crutch

Solidarity?
What choice have we now?
Justice is the one staff for freedom's flag
How can we share with the enemy our voice?
Violence comes from the mind's core

If unshackling were a song
I'd slide my palm on skin
And watch it trail to air

                              Forgive my days of fullness, he prayed
                    In this land of filch, let my wares be witness
                        Sokar, bless these hands with flourish
                       As my heart is weighed against a feather

The bones of possibility, laid to rest
Stratum, the root's architecture
Isis' map floats in an ocean sweep
And what can we exhume from this great distance?

Every time he looks to this sea
He is reminded of his own humanity
With every shuffled step
He recalls everything that is left

Intrinsic is her name
Isis' calling buried dead
Antiquity, enigmatic wonder
History a chafe of surface and burn
Cracked light into woven earth

Who desiccated the darkness
In the nation of wont?
Shading their day from the pelagic road
Stripped the bark of verdure from the day

Their bodies have absorbed this poison
Flanked by an iridescence
Fraught by the way of home

If cartography were a bird
Would she dot her notes on a river bottom?
Would she croon her maps on a mountain ridge?
Would her cadence lead us home?

Tekla tells a story of come and gone
Carves the mask of dignity
Makes a place for fire

Nefer is the land
Stolen in her grace
Made part by the legacy of hunger
The flock of wingless birds

What if we were free
Like the facilities of Africa
The taking of an anomaly
The mapping of rout
Assembled at the edge of the desert

Harmony makes a road
To the victim's haven
We must not tell of wisdom's knots

He seeks refuge in the shade of acacia
Stolen on the land of sand
Loose is the root in decadence

From this canopy of thirst
Release comes
This is sovereignty
This is the story of hope

> Like the order of a midnight office
> Begin believing
> Say loudly everything that need be said
> Train your feet to walk the night

If every wanderer touched the sky
Was made full by Sah's direction
Spoken in another language
Premonition would be their freedom

In the hail of lead
We were made to understand our veins
Forget the vestiture of desire
Cloak ourselves in an impending life

From the sinister gaze of the Atlantic
Its mouth curling with foam
Swept between a desolation
Isis found her way

Every memory
Became a home of its own
Despite the illusion
A reminder that nothing stagnant could be held

> This skin he remembered
> Borrowed from the hide of his kin
> Tekla carried on this wanting

NOTES:

Sokar: An ancient Ancient Egyptian god of the necropolis in Memphis, Sokar is often shown with a human body and the head of a hawk. Although his origins are obscure, he is believed to have been a patron of craftsmen as well as a god of fertility.

Nefer: In ancient Egyptian, the hieroglyphic sign most often depicted to mean "goodness" or "beauty."

Sah: The Ancient Egyptian god who presided over the constellation commonly called Orion.

Javier Sicilia

Lo abierto

A nosotros, que erguidos caminamos
como si en ese gesto se ocultara el sino de nuestra condición,
no el animal que avanza a ras de tierra hacia lo Abierto,
un atrás y adelante en el acontecer del infinito;
no el árbol que enraizado
—la boca entre la tierra,
el sexo contra el viento—
habita el puro espacio de su inmovilidad;
no el ángel, demasiado perfecto en su belleza,
esencia fabricada de espacioave de luz suspendida en lo eterno;
sino nosotros que avanzamos a tientas
entre el cielo y la tierra, aterrados de muerte,
excavados de huecos;
a nosotros, *viatores*
—que a la vez anhelamos la tierra y lo celestey no estamos en paz con nosotros mismos—,
sólo el amor nos salva de la angustiosa fuga hacia adelante,
como si en los contornos de lo amado lo Abierto se cerraray el hueco de la carne
encontrara el reposo en lo creado
y no viera la muerte,
sino un allá anunciado,
contenido en los límites del cuerpo.
Los amantes lo saben,
ellos que tan cercanos uno al otro
se miran asombrados en lo Abierto que sus ojos descubren en sus ojos.
Mas ni el uno ni el otro lo franquean
y regresan al mundo.
¿Será tal vez el miedo al llamado infinito
o la dulce nostalgia de quedarse por siempre en lo creado
que nunca los retiene?
O quizás ese sea nuestro sitio,
el lugar de lo eterno que nos corresponde:
contemplar y sentir el infinito arropado en la carne,
en ese mutuo darse el uno al otro,
mientras la lenta fuga hacia lo Abierto nos permite habitar la duración,ese ya, pero aún no
que lo amantes viven al rozarse la piel;

esa eterna presenciaque nos hace presentes en el tiempo inasiblecomo una tenue grieta
en la alba porcelana de lo Abierto.

Sicilia

What Is Open

To us, who walk upright,
as if the fate of our condition would be covered by that gesture,
not the animal that advances low to the ground toward what is Open,
a backwards and forwards in the happening of the infinite;
not the tree that rooted
—its mouth within the earth,
its sex against the wind—
inhabits the pure space of your immobility;
not the angel, too perfect in its beauty,
an essence made of space,
bird of light suspended in the eternal;
but we who advance gropingly
between heaven and earth, terrified of death,
hollowed with holes;

to us, viatores,
—who yearn for both the earth and the heavenly
and aren't at peace with ourselves—,
only love saves us from our anxious flight forward,
as if in the contours of what is loved what is Open would close
and the hollowness of flesh would find repose in what is created
and would not see its death,
but rather a proclaimed beyond,
contained within the limits of the body.

Lovers know it,
those, so close to one another, who
look amazed into the Openness that their eyes discover in their eyes.
But neither one or the other cross into it
and they return to the world.
Could it perhaps be the fear of the infinite call
or the sweet nostalgia of forever residing in what is created
that never restrains them?

Or maybe that is our place,
the spot of the eternal that corresponds us:
to contemplate and feel the infinite wrapped in the flesh,
in that mutual giving of one to the other,
while the slow flight toward what is Open allows us to inhabit the duration,
that already but not yet
that the lovers live at grazing skin;
that eternal presence
that makes us present in ungraspable time
like a tenuous crack
in the porcelain alb of the Open.

Translated from the Spanish by David Shook

Richard Siken

Detail of the Fire

A man with a bandage is in the middle of something.

Everyone understands this. Everyone wants a battlefield.
Red. And a little more red.

Accidents never happen when the room is empty.
Everyone understands this. Everyone needs a place.

People like to think war means something.

What can you learn from your opponent? More than you think.
Who will master this love? Love might be the wrong word.

Let's admit, without apology, what we do to each other.
We know who our enemies are. We know.

Landscape with a Blur of Conquerors

To have a thought, there must be an object—
the field is empty, sloshed with gold, a hayfield thick
with sunshine. There must be an object so land
a man there, solid on his feet, on solid ground, in
a field fully flooded, enough light to see him clearly,

the light on his skin and bouncing off his skin.
He's easy to desire since there's not much to him,
vague and smeary in his ochers, in his umbers,
burning in the open field. Forget about his insides,
his plumbing and his furnaces, put a thing in his hand

and be done with it. No one wants to know what's
in his head. It should be enough. To make something
beautiful should be enough. It isn't. It should be.
The smear of his head—I paint it out, I paint it in
again. I ask it what it wants. *I want to be a cornerstone*,

says the head. *Let's kill something.* Land a man in a
landscape and he'll try to conquer it. Make him
handsome and you're a fascist, make him ugly and
you're saying nothing new. The conqueror suits up
and takes the field, his horse already painted in

beneath him. What do you do with a man like that?
While you are deciding, more men ride in. The hand
sings *weapon*. The mind says *tool*. The body swerves
in the service of the mind, which is evidence of
the mind but not actual proof. More conquerors.

They swarm the field and their painted flags unfurl.
Crown yourself with leaves and stake your claim
before something smears up the paint. I turned away
from darkness to see daylight, to see what would
happen. What happened? What does a man want?

Power. The men spread, the thought extends. I paint

them out, I paint them in again. A blur of forces.
Why take more than we need? Because we can.
Deep footprint, it leaves a hole. You'd break your
heart to make it bigger, so why not crack your skull

when the mind swells. A thought bigger than your
own head. Try it. Seriously. Cover more ground.
I thought of myself as a city and I liked my lips.
I thought of myself as a nation and I wrung my hands,
I put a thing in your hand. Will you defend yourself?

From me, I mean. Let's kill something. The mind
moves forward, the paint layers up: glop glop and
shellac. I shovel the color into our faces, I shovel our
faces into our faces. They look like me. I move them
around. I prefer to blame others, it's easier. King me.

Jane Springer

Salt Hill

I was born in a Tennessee sanatorium hours after my mother's father died & I know how the womb becomes a salt-sea grave.

I was born in the last seconds of small crops & small change rained down on the collection plate's felt palate & I know

the soul's barn debt to past generations, too.

Outside, ditchfuls of chicory flashed in the after-rain sun as melancholia's purple scent rose & its steepled fog distilled in Tennessee hills.

& I know I'm not supposed to be here on account of all those crazy aunts & I know great grandma was five

when her Cherokee mother died & her daddy dumped her on the red clay curb of an Arkansas reservation then drove away in a wagon—

how she just strode the fields of milkweed back to Tennessee & married her cousin.

When I was five I drowned a fly in a piepan of water then spooned it out & heaped a hill of salt on its still body until I could hear a buzz again (as if within a belly)

& I know the rush of the resurrected.

I was born in the last decade of small town girls wearing white gloves to funerals.

As an infant my boy quit suckling long enough to wave to my mother's ghost— who used to drift in the doorway of the hours.

& at three he told me at my age he had red hair & broke his neck falling off a runaway horse—I know

                      the rocking chair's set too close to the edge of the porch.

Brian Teare

Genius Loci

(*Oakland*)

Make it
the place
it was then,

so full it split
vision to live
there in winter

so late & wet
abundance
toppled toward

awful—birds
of paradise
a profusion

the ripe colors
of anodized
metal; in gutters

umbrellas
smashed
like pigeons,

bent ribs bright
among black
slack fluttering;

camellias'
pink imagoes
dropping

into water
& rotting,
sweet stink—

& did not
stop :
the inundated

eye, over-
populous
urban eye,

the whole
place, to look
at it, was

a footprint
in January :
everywhere

cloudy water
rising to fill in
the outlines,

& meanwhile
indoors differed
by degree

alone : without
love, loosed
from God,

there were
lovers & touch
rushing in

to redraw
your boundaries
constantly

because
it was a tune
you kept

getting wrong,
the refrain
of what it meant

to live alone,
months of that
and then

•

sudden summer, sheer release, streets all cigarettes & sashay,
   balls-out tube tops, low-riders & belly fat, the girls on the block

all like *Oh no she didn't*, and girl, she did, she was mad skills
   with press-ons & a cell phone telling him where to stick it, a kid

on her hip, just like that, summer, sheer beauty & lip gloss
   that smelled like peaches, & you going to the store for whiskey

& condoms like everyone else on a hot, long afternoon
   so long & hot it would just be sunburn to walk anywhere if it weren't also

a pleasure, thoughtless & shiftless & horny & drunk,
   just someone thinking summer wasn't up to anything deep, & lo

there he was, his punk ass pink as a Viking in a tight
   wifebeater & lingering by the public pool, drinking beer so sly

it didn't look illegal, & he wasn't a good idea but
   did you have a light? & it seemed the whole summer went like that,

taking fire out of your pocket & giving it away, a ditty
   you could whistle it was so cliché, like the numbers they gave you after

& you never called, the number of swollen nodes of the kissing
    colds you got & later the number to call to get tested, the number of the bus

to the clinic, the number they gave you when they asked
    you to wait, the number of questions asked, number of partners, number

of risks, number of previous tests, the number of pricks
    —one—to draw the blood, the number of minutes you waited before

results, & then you decided you had to get the tune right,
    the how to live it so it doesn't kill you, to take a number & wait in the long line

of the city's bankrupt humanism like the bus that never comes
    no matter how long you wait, & the grocery bag breaking, & if you were going

to sing that one, the one that sounds like all I got is bruised
    tomatoes, broken glass & dirty bread & no one waiting at home, would you

•

start with *genius*,
as in, the spirit
of a place?,

& *small*, as in
of the back, wet
in heat

& the urge
to touch him
there, skin

just visible
between his jeans
& t-shirt,

to see if
he's sweating,
to see

if he feels
what you feel?,
& if he does,

is that all
the spirit the place
will give,

a small thing
shared, just
a phrase, not

a whole song,
but something
to build on?,

& if it isn't bread
& if it sure
ain't tomatoes

it isn't empty,
is it, like the signage
you walk by

that fronts
the Lakeside
Church of Practical

Christianity,
hawking
a knowledge of God

so modest
it seems trivial?,
& it isn't ever,

is it, the how
to live it
so it doesn't

kill you,
the where
to touch it,

the when
will genius
sing your name

so it sounds
like a place
you can live?

Truth Thomas

The Bloody Red Wheelbarrow
after WCW

so much is built
upon

a black mother's
child

pooling blood in
streets

shot by the white
police.

Urban Warming

Stoned by no Rosetta,
merchants allowed through the fence
learn to misspeak "black speak,"

in Edgar's harbor village,
at HipHop Fish & Chicken
on Route number 4 x 10.

"Baby Girl" becomes XX.
"My Man" assumes all XY.

For salt & pepper curls,
& baby stroller crowds,
their broadcast is the same:

"Baby Girl, your Diabetes
is ready." "My Man, your
Hypertension is up."

They know their audience:
french fried lives, french fried
luck, french fried us.

They know corner markets
of cornered markets, seldom
scale the wall. Their shit

is always hot. Their shit is
always cheap. Their shit is

always landmark of poison
in pens, along with: windows
wearing boards, hubcaps

leaning curbs, the sound of
"bitch," the sound of "mother-
fucker," the sound of "niggah"

sounding off, projectile vomiting
from children's lips—our hush
puppy young, made beasts

behind these bars. Some days
you will see them, dirt bike
knights, riding Edmonson

Avenue, armor-less. They are
wheelies, jousting against traffic,
wheelies, jousting against stop

lights, gas tanks bleeding out
on stretchers, as sirens serenade,
metal flies hover. There are

skeletons of chickens scattered on
the ground. There are meeting bones
of children fractured in the street,

cordoned off.

This is urban warming. This is
underwear in exhibition, pants
saddened to sag, hanging off ass

cracks, like wet clothes on a line.
This is the ecology of locks, since
our country is locks, since our

color is locks, since this block is
locked. When your order is up,
you will eat anything tossed inside

the cage.

Brian Turner

Sadiq

> *It is a condition of wisdom in the archer to be patient*
> *because when the arrow leaves the bow, it returns no more.*
> — Sa'di

It should make you shake and sweat,
nightmare you, strand you in a desert
of irrevocable desolation, the consequences
seared into the vein, no matter what adrenaline
feeds the muscle its courage, no matter
what god shines down on you, no matter
what crackling pain and anger
you carry in your fists, my friend,
it should break your heart to kill.

Phantom Noise

There is this ringing hum this
bullet-borne language ringing
shell-fall and static this late-night
ringing of threadwork and carpet ringing
hiss and steam this wing-beat
of rotors and tanks broken
bodies ringing in steel humming these
voices of dust these years ringing
rifles in Babylon rifles in Sumer
ringing these children their gravestones
and candy their limbs gone missing their
static-borne television their ringing
this eardrum this rifled symphonic this
ringing of midnight in gunpowder and oil this
brake pad gone useless this muzzle-flash singing this
threading of bullets in muscle and bone this ringing
hum this ringing hum this
ringing

Sarah Vap

bluebells. blueballs. ballerinas.

corn on the mountainside, a rhomboid-swath

a thousand years old, not like grandfather's neverending
row in nebraska's
heartland... *give his children something*—trafficking in sueños like some

androgynous florida. grandfather'd say it won't matter in a hundred years, and,
shit or get off the pot.   he'd give you anything—phantasmagoria, extra-

terrestrial—no matter how grandmother's shawls and eyeshadows were the cardinal

point for certainty.   if lost, we're to walk straight down one row until
we arrived at the railroad tracks, and wait—this alage

in the incan shower,
puma-face where the sun hits the limestone labyrinth

every morning, and our morning's affectation.

ANNIE WON

⋏ ORIENTATION

What About Following Streams?

record of all angles
we can always tell how far
lies the spot from which we
started.

The more you and I learn
we realize that no way of
thinking or doing can be
trusted

the of
ten fatal tendency of

well settled country

keeping to the higher sides

if we can keep going long enough

In real wilderness,

something else entirely,

Suppose we can

Who Should

174   LOCKED HORN PRESS

ORIENTATION

▓▓▓▓▓▓ directly ▓▓▓ in the straightest possible line ▓▓▓▓▓▓ ▓▓▓▓▓▓▓▓▓▓▓▓▓ easily and safely ▓▓▓▓▓▓▓▓▓▓▓▓▓▓▓▓▓▓▓▓▓▓▓▓▓▓▓ getting a dead branch in the eye.

▓▓▓▓▓ the path that follows a straight line

▓▓▓▓▓▓▓▓▓▓▓▓▓▓▓▓▓ exactly south by the needle. ▓▓▓▓ we've dropped down to the flat, we're in ▓▓▓ thick ▓▓▓▓▓ ▓▓▓▓▓▓▓▓▓▓▓▓▓ we have to get down and crawl. ▓▓▓▓▓▓▓▓▓▓▓▓▓▓▓▓▓▓▓

READ AMERICA(S): AN ANTHOLOGY 175

WON

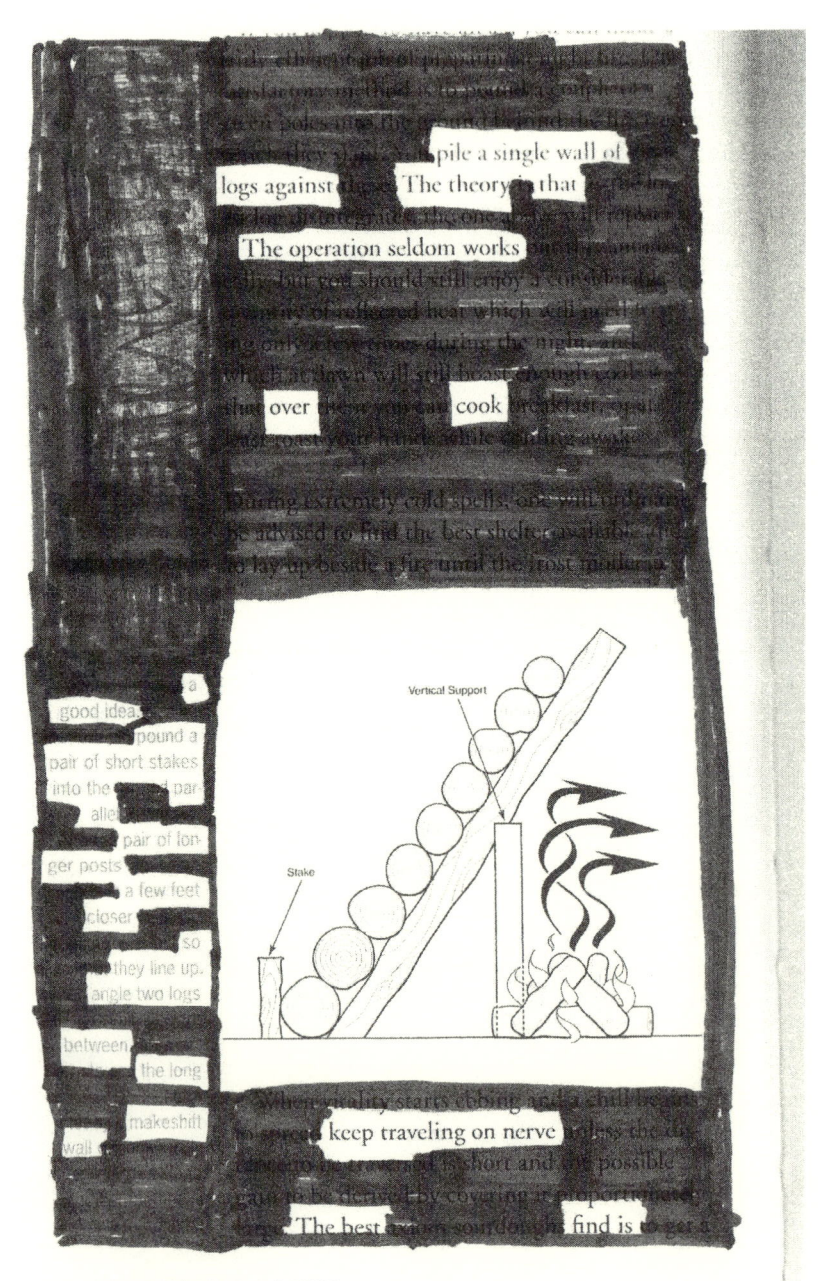

pile a single wall of
logs against

The operation seldom works

over   cook

a
good idea.
pound a
pair of short stakes
into the
pair of lon-
ger posts
a few feet
closer
so
they line up.
angle two logs

between
the long

makeshift
keep traveling on nerve

146 HOW TO STAY ALIVE IN THE WOODS

Won

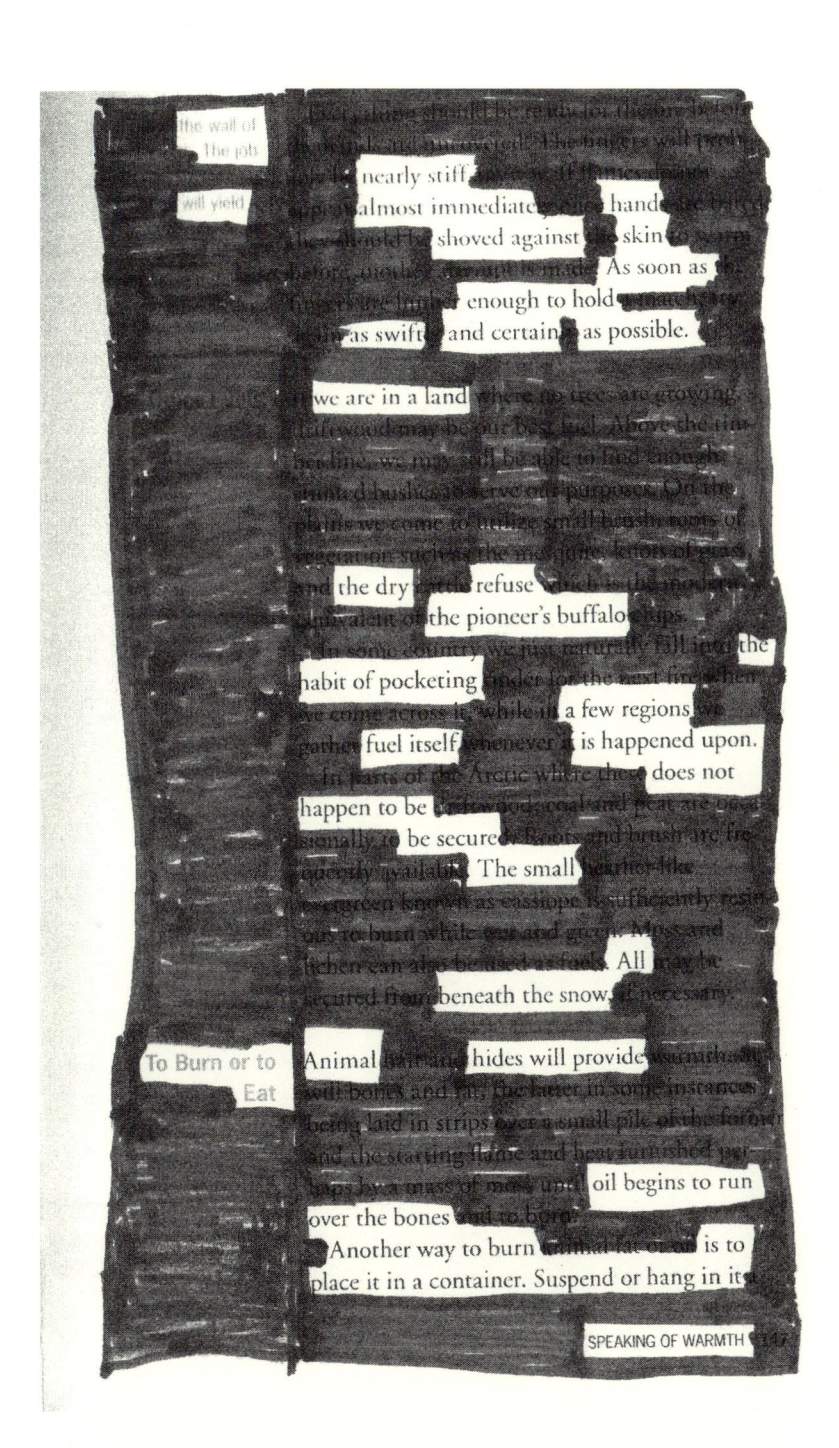

the wall of
the job
will yield

nearly stiff almost immediate hand shoved against the skin As soon as enough to hold as swift and certain as possible.

we are in a land

the dry refuse the pioneer's buffalo

habit of pocketing a few regions fuel itself is happened upon.

happen to be be secured The small

To Burn or to
Eat

Animal hides will provide oil begins to run over the bones Another way to burn is to place it in a container. Suspend or hang in it

SPEAKING OF WARMTH

Monika Zobel

The Immigrant Searches the Map for Countries Larger Than His Palm

I was born in the first century of guilt.
Between shattered church bells, we played

in a cemetery of wishbone homes. Ghosts had no
middle names. Every night I curled

on a bench with the moan of a cast iron stove.
In November meatless heads of cabbage

churned through the kitchen, chatter
of chickens before the axe guillotined

the fogged glass. I counted the pulse, the pulse
of termites between floorboards. Memorized

the wall cracks like borders drawn by clouds.
When the house flooded with the river's excess—

tired of drawing borders—my parents drowned
their wool coats in the Rhine. Mold bloomed

in the moist crevices between our eyelashes.
Flying over the Atlantic, water swallowed

the scent of home—rust and cinnamon.
The itinerary was stamped in our palms at birth.

CONTRIBUTOR BIOGRAPHIES

Elmaz Abinader is an author and a performer. Her most recent poetry collection, *This House, My Bones*, was the Editor's Selection for 2014 from Willow Books/Aquarius. Her books include a memoir: *Children of the Roojme, A Family's Journey from Lebanon*, a book of poetry, *In the Country of My Dreams...* which won the PEN Oakland Josephine Miles Award. Her plays include *Ramadan Moon*, *32 Mohammeds*, and *Country of Origin*. Elmaz is one of the co-founders of The Voices of Our Nations Arts Foundation (VONA/Voices), a writing workshop for writers-of-color. She teaches at Mills College, is an instructor at the Oakland Y, and lives in Oakland with her husband Anthony Byers. www.elmazabinader.com

Elizabeth Acevedo was born and raised in New York City and her poetry is infused with her Dominican parents' bolero and her beloved city's tough grit. She holds a BA in Performing Arts from The George Washington University and an MFA in Creative Writing from the University of Maryland. With over twelve years of performance experience, Acevedo has graced stages nationally and internationally including renowned venues such as The Lincoln Center, Madison Square Garden, the Kennedy Center of the Performing Arts, and South Africa's State Theatre. Acevedo is a National Slam Champion. She lives in Washington D.C. and has been published or has poems forthcoming in *The Acentos Review*, *The Ostrich Review*, *Split This Rock*, *Callaloo*, *Poet Lore* and *The Notre Dame Review*.

Acevedo is a Cave Canem Fellow, Cantomundo Fellow, and participant of the Callaloo Writer's Workshop. Her book of poems, *Beastgirl & Other Origin Myths* is forthcoming (YesYes Books).

James E. Allman, Jr.'s credentials—degrees in biology and business—qualify him for an altogether different trade. However, he easily tires of the dissected and austerely economized. He is a dabbler with an expensive photography-habit and a poetry-dependency. Nominated for three Pushcart Prizes, his work appears, or is forthcoming, in *Black Warrior Review*, *Los Angeles Review*, *Nimrod*, *Prairie Schooner*, *Sugar House Review*, and *Third Coast*, among others. He's written reviews for Rattle as well as other journals, blogs and sundries and is the co-founder of an artist community called *Continuum*.

Hari Alluri is a poet, community facilitator and co-founding editor of Locked Horn Press. His writing appears in journals, anthologies, online and in the forthcoming chapbook and book *The Promise of Rust* (Mouthfeel) and *The Flayed City* (Kaya).

Kofi Awoonor is a Ghanaian poet and novelist, born at Wheta in the Volta Region, and educated at the University of Ghana. Before moving to London in 1967, he was Director of the Ghana Film Corporation. He taught both at the University of London and at the Stony Brook campus of New York State University, where he became Chairman of Comparative Literature. On release from prison for an alleged connection with an attempted coup, he became Professor of English at Cape Coast in 1976. His literary reputation rests chiefly on the poems in *Rediscovery* (1964) and *Night of My Blood* (1971), both of which adapt techniques from poetry by Ewe dirge singers to explore the modern African psyche. His translations of Ewe poetry, much of it somber and tragic in tone, appear in *Guardians of the Sacred Word* (1974). Richly imagistic in texture, and politically allegorical, his novel *This Earth, My Brother: An Allegorical Tale of Africa* (1970) focuses on the search for meaning by a lawyer on the brink of a nervous breakdown. Other poetry collections include *Ride Me, Memory* (1973) and *The House by the Sea* (1978). *The Breast of the Earth* (1975), a major work of criticism, surveys the history, culture, and literature of Africa south of the Sahara.

Sherwin Bitsui is the author of *Flood Song* (Copper Canyon Press) and *Shapeshift* (University of Arizona Press). He Diné is of the Bįį'bítóó'nii' Tódi'chii'nii clan and is born for the Tlizilłani' clan. He is from White Cone, Arizona on the Navajo Reservation. His honors include the 2011 Lannan Literary Fellowship, a Native Arts & Culture Foundation Fellowship for Literature, a PEN Open Book Award, an American Book Award and a Whiting Writers Award. Bitsui lives in San Diego, California and teaches at the MFA writing programs of both San Diego State University and IAIA MFA in Creative Writing in Santa Fe, New Mexico.

Mario Bojórquez is a self-taught writer and poet from Los Mochis, Sinaloa, Mexico. He is the author of several books of poetry, essays and translations. His work has won many awards including the State Prize of Literature of Baja California (1991), the Clemencia Isaura National Poetry Award (1995) (1996), the Enriqueta Ochoa National Poetry Prize (1996), the Abigael Bohórquez Poetry Prize (1996), the Aguascalientes National Poetry Prize (2007), and the José Revueltas Literary Essay Fine Arts Prize (2010). He recently received the Alhambra American Poetry Prize (2012), awarded by the Council of the Alhambra and Generalife and the International Poetry Festival in Granada, Spain. He has received scholarships for young artists from the National Institute of Fine Arts, FONCA, and State Funds for Culture and Arts of Sinaloa and Baja California.

Daniel Borzutzky's books and chapbooks include, among others, *The Performance of Becoming Human* (2016); *In the Murmurs of the Rotten Carcass Economy* (2015); *Memories of my Overdevelopment* (2015); *Bedtime Stories For The End of the World!* (2015), *Data Bodies* (2013), *The Book of Interfering Bodies* (2011), and *The Ecstasy of Capitulation* (2007). He has translated Raúl Zurita's *The Country of Planks* (2015) and *Song for his Disappeared Love* (2010), and Jaime Luis Huenún's *Port Trakl* (2008). His work has been supported by the Illinois Arts Council, the National Endowment for the Arts, and the Pen/Heim Translation Fund. He lives in Chicago.

Ana Bosch received her Bachelors degree at San Diego State University (SDSU) in Televison, Film, and New Media with an emphasis in Critical Studies. Following her studies in this field she returned to SDSU to pursue her Graduate degree as a candidate in the MFA Creative Writing Program. While in her studies in the MFA program she has gained knowledge in translating poetry. She hopes to have more of her poems published so that they may be available for all to enjoy.

Geoff Bouvier's first book of poetry, *Living Room*, won the 2005 APR/Honickman Prize and was published by Copper Canyon Press. In 2009, he served as the poet-in-residence at the University of California-Berkeley. His second book, *Glass Harmonica*, was published in 2011 by Quale Press. He holds an MFA from Bard College, and is currently a PhD candidate in poetry at Florida State University.

Derrick Weston Brown holds an MFA in Creative Writing from American University. He has studied poetry under Dr. Tony Medina at Howard University and Cornelius Eady at American University. He is a graduate of the Cave Canem Summer workshop for black poets and the VONA summer workshop. His work has appeared in such literary journals as *The Little Patuxent Review, Mythium, The Tidal Basin Review, DrumVoices, The Columbia Poetry Review*, and the online journals *Beltway Poetry Quarterly, Howard University's Amistad, LocusPoint, MiPOesias, Vinyl Poetry, Borderline, ThisMag* and most recently had a poem go viral through *Colorlines*. He's also performed at many poetry venues around the country, from The Nuyorican Poets Café and The Bowery in NYC to Beyond Baroque in Los Angeles. He is a former publications advocate and book buyer for a bookstore which was operated by the social justice nonprofit Teaching for Change, and which located within the restaurant, bar, coffee shop and performance space known as Busboys and Poets. He has appeared on Al-Jazeera America's "The Stream," and VOA (Voice of America), Rwanda Radio.

As the first Poet-in-Residence of Busboys and Poets, he is the founder and host of The Nine on the Ninth, the very first and longest running poetry series of the Busboys and Poets, and currently helps coordinate the poetry programming at the 14th & V Street location. He teaches Poetry and Creative Writing to a small but gifted class of high schoolers at Emerson Preparatory School. He was the visiting Writer-in-Residence of Howard County Maryland for the 2012-2013 academic year and the 2015 Spring Semester Writer-in-Residence of The University of The District of Columbia. He is also a participating DC area author for the PEN/Faulkner foundation's Writers-in-Schools program. He's performed at such esteemed venues as The Nuyorican Poets' Cafe and the Bowery. He has lead workshops and performed at Georgetown University, George Washington University and Chicago State. He has appeared on Al-Jazeera and NPR as well. In May of 2014 he was also the recipient of a Maryland State Arts Council Individual Artist Grant. He is a native of Charlotte, North Carolina, and resides in Mount Rainier, Maryland. His debut collection of poetry, entitled *Wisdom Teeth*, was released in April 2011 on Busboys and Poets Press/PM Press.

Jericho Brown is the recipient of a Whiting Writers Award and fellowships from the Radcliffe Institute for Advanced Study at Harvard University and the National Endowment for the Arts. His poems have appeared in *The New Republic, The New Yorker*, and *The Best American Poetry*. His first book, *Please*, won the American Book Award, and his second book, *The New Testament*, won the Anisfield-Wolf Book Award and the Thom Gunn Award, and it was named one of the best books of the year by *Library Journal, Coldfront*, and the Academy of American Poets. He is an associate professor in English and Creative Writing at Emory University in Atlanta.

Alí Calderón is a poet, novelist and essayist born in Mexico City in 1982. He holds a PhD in Linguistics and Literature, and is a professor at the Autonomous University of Puebla. He has contributed articles and poems in *Alforja, Dosfilos, Luvina, Reverse, Journal of Contemporary Mexican Literature* (University of Texas at El Paso) and *Inland*. He is a co-founder of the publishing house and the magazine *Poetry Circle*, www.circulodepoesia.com. He was a fellow of the Foundation for Mexican Letters, 2003-2004. Inter Award (BUAP / UDLA / UIA) Test the state of Puebla, 2003. National Poetry Prize Ramon Lopez Velarde, 2004. Winner of the Latin American Poetry Prize Benemérito de las Américas, 2007, for *Ser en el mundo*. Part of his work is included in several anthologies, including *Los mejores poemas mexicanos* (2005); *Más vale sollozar afilando la navaja* (2004) and *Poesía ante la incertidumbre, antología de nuevos poetas en español* (2011).

Grady Chambers was born and raised in Chicago, Illinois, and currently lives in Syracuse, New York. Work of his can be found in *Ninth Letter, Barrow Street, Cimarron Review, Devil's Lake, The Rumpus*, and elsewhere. He is a graduate of the MFA Program in Creative Writing at Syracuse University, and a first-year Stegner Fellow at Stanford University.

Nadia Chaney is an Indo-Canadian poet, performer and community arts facilitator. Her poetry has recently appeared or will appear with *Naugatuck River Review*, Terrain.org, and *Flycatcher Journal*.

Jennifer Chang is the author of *The History of Anonymity* (University of Georgia Press, 2008). Her poems have appeared in *Kenyon Review, Poetry, The Nation, New England Review, A Public Space*, and *Best American Poetry 2012* and she has written essays on poetry for *The Believer, Boston Review, Los Angeles Review of Books* and *The Volta*. She co-chairs the advisory board of Kundiman, an Asian American poetry organization and is an assistant professor of English and Creative Writing at the George Washington University.

Briceida Cuevas Cob is a Mayan poet born on on July 12, 1969, in Tepakan, Calkiní, Campeche, México. After completing her studies in accounting and administration, her love of language arts led her to participate in various creative writing workshops with writers such as Carlos Montemayor, Carlos Illescas, Juan Bañuelos, amongst others. She is currently perusing a degree in Creative Writing at the Universidad Autónoma de la Ciudad de México. Her poetry has appeared in several literary magazines and newspapers in Quintana Roo, Campeche, Yucatán, and Mexico City, and her poems have been translated into languages such as French, Dutch, Catalan, English, Italian and Russian. She has given lectures and participated in academic conferences both in Mexico, and abroad, and is the author of several poetry books: *U yok'ol awat peek'* (*El quejido del perro / The dog's moan*) (1995), *Je' bix k'iin* (*Como el sol / Like The Sun*) (1998), *Ti' u billil in nook'* (*Del dobladillo de mi ropa / From My Clothes' Hem*) (2008). In 1996, she received a scholarship from the Fondo Nacional para la Cultura y las Artes para Escritores en Lenguas Indígenas (National Fund for the Culture and Arts for Writers in Indigenous

Languages). In that year, Cuevas Cob wrote a book on the daily life of Mayan women. She is a founding member of the Asociación de Lenguas Indígenas (Association of Writers in Indigenous Languages) in Mexico, was a judge for the Nezahualcóyotl Prize in 2002, and was selected as part of the delegation of Mexican writers to attend la Feria del Salón del Libro in Paris, France, (2009). In May of 2012 Briceida Cuevas Cob was chosen as corresponding academic in Campeche by the Mexican Academy of the Language, entered the Sistema Nacional de Creadores de Arte in 2009 and again in 2013, and was selected as a judge for the Premio de Literatura Indígena de América (PLIA) (Indigenous Literature Prize of America) in 2014.

Karla Cordero is a 2015 recipient of the Spoken Word Immersion Fellowship from the Loft Literary Center in Minneapolis, Minnesota. Cordero is a contributing editor for *Poetry International* and founding editor of *Spit Journal*. Her work has been published in *Word Riot, Toe Good Poetry, The Acentos Review*, and elsewhere. Cordero's first chapbook, *Grasshoppers Before Gods*, was just released from Dancing Girl Press..

Cynthia Cruz is the author of four collections of poems: *Ruin* (Alice James Books, 2006), The *Glimmering Room* (Four Way Books, 2012), *Wunderkammer* (Four Way Books, 2014), and *How the End Begins* (Four Way Books, 2016). Her essays and art writings have been published in *The Los Angeles Review of Books, The American Poetry Review, Guernica*, and *The Rumpus*. She is currently at work on two poetry anthologies: one of Latina poets and the other, a collection of poetry by female poets around the issue of consumption and nourishment. She is a regular contributor for the art journal *Hyperallergic*. She has received fellowships from Yaddo and the MacDowell Colony as well as a Hodder Fellowship from Princeton University. She has an MFA from Sarah Lawrence College in writing and an MFA in Art Criticism & Writing from the School of Visual Arts. In the fall, she will be pursuing a PhD in German Studies at Rutgers University. She teaches at Sarah Lawrence College and is currently at work on a collection of essays on language and iterations of silence.

Kyle Dargan is the author of four collections of poetry, *Honest Engine* (2015), *Logorrhea Dementia* (2010), *Bouquet of Hungers* (2007) and *The Listening* (2003), all published by the University of Georgia Press. For his work, he has received the Cave Canem Poetry Prize, the Hurston/Wright Legacy Award, and grants from the D.C. Commission on the Arts and Humanities. Dargan has partnered with the President's Committee on the Arts and Humanities to produce poetry programming at the White House and Library of Congress. He's worked with and supports a number of youth writing organizations, such as 826DC, Writopia Lab and the Young Writers Workshop. He is currently an Associate Professor of literature and director of creative writing at American University, as well as the founder and editor of *POST NO ILLS* magazine. Originally from Newark, New Jersey, Dargan is a graduate of Saint Benedict's Prep, The University of Virginia and Indiana University.

Meg Day is the 2015-2016 recipient of the Amy Lowell Poetry Travelling Scholarship, a 2013 recipient of an NEA Fellowship in Poetry, and the author of *Last Psalm at Sea Level* (Barrow Street 2014), winner of the Barrow Street Poetry Prize and the Publishing Triangle's Audre Lorde Award. Day is Assistant Professor of English & Creative Writing at Franklin & Marshall College and lives in Lancaster, PA. www.megday.com

Sunshine Dempsey received her MFA in Poetry from Colorado State University in 2010 and her MA in English from Lynchburg College, Virginia, in 2014. Her work has appeared in several literary journals including *Matter, Hayden's Ferry Review, ditch*, and *Hotel Amerika*, and she was a finalist in the New Michigan Press/DIAGRAM chapbook competition in 2012. Currently, Sunshine lives in Columbia, South Carolina, where she is pursuing her PhD in American Literature at the University of South Carolina.

Natalie Diaz was born and raised in the Fort Mojave Indian Village in Needles, California, on the banks of the Colorado River. She is Mojave and an enrolled member of the Gila River Indian Tribe. Her first poetry collection, *When My Brother Was an Aztec*, was published by Copper Canyon Press. Her second book will be published by Copper Canyon Press in 2016. She is a 2012 Lannan Literary Fellow and a 2012 Native Arts Council Foundation Artist Fellow. In 2014, she was awarded a Bread Loaf Fellowship, as well as the Holmes National Poetry Prize and a Hodder Fellowship, both from Princeton University, a Civatella Ranieri Foundation Residency, and a US Artists Ford Fellowship.

Diaz teaches at the Institute of American Indian Arts Low Rez MFA program and lives in Mohave Valley, Arizona, where she directs the Fort Mojave Language Recovery Program, working with the last remaining speakers at Fort Mojave to teach and revitalize the Mojave language.

Camille Dungy is author of *Smith Blue* (Southern Illinois University Press, 2011), winner of the 2010 Crab Orchard Open Book Prize, *Suck on the Marrow* (Red Hen Press, 2010), and *What to Eat, What to Drink, What to Leave for Poison* (Red Hen Press, 2006).

Dungy is editor of *Black Nature: Four Centuries of African American Nature Poetry* (UGA, 2009), co-editor of *From the Fishouse: An Anthology of Poems that Sing, Rhyme, Resound, Syncopate, Alliterate, and Just Plain Sound Great* (Persea, 2009), and assistant editor of *Gathering Ground: A Reader Celebrating Cave Canem's First Decade* (University of Michigan Press, 2006). Dungy has received fellowships from the National Endowment for the Arts, the Virginia Commission for the Arts, Cave Canem, the Dana Award, and Bread Loaf.

She is a two-time recipient of the Northern California Book Award (2010 and 2011), a Silver Medal Winner in the California Book Award (2011), and a two-time NAACP Image Award nominee (2010 and 2011). She was a 2011 finalist for the Balcones Prize, and her books have been shortlisted for the 2011 Foreword Magazine Book of the Year Award, the PEN Center USA 2007 Literary Award, and the Library of Virginia 2007 Literary Award. Recently a Professor in the Creative Writing Department at San Francisco State University, Dungy is now a Professor in the English Department at Colorado State University. Her poems and essays have been published widely in anthologies and print and online journals.

Chicano Americano poet, **Jesus Antonio Esparza**, received his MFA from San Diego State University, where he built upon his skills as a Hip Hop artist. With a creative backbone of two full length hip hop albums, his work as a performance poet helped shape the foundation of community based artist space Voz Alta in San Diego, California, which continues to thrive and highlight local artists. Esparza's work is a direct reflection of his experiences straddling and/or struggling with two worlds, two cultures, American and Mexican.

Jill Alexander Essbaum is the author of several collections of poetry and her work has appeared in *The Best American Poetry*, as well as its sister anthology, *The Best American Erotic Poems, 1800-Present*. She is the winner of the Bakeless Poetry Prize and recipient of two NEA literature fellowships. A member of the core faculty at the University of California, Riverside's Palm Desert Low-Residency MFA program, she lives and writes in Austin, Texas.

Tarfia Faizullah is the author of *Register of Eliminated Villages* (Graywolf 2017) and *Seam* (SIU 2014), the 2015 winner of a VIDA Award, GLCA New Writers' Award, and the Milton Kessler First Book Award. Recent poems appear in *Poetry Magazine, jubilat, New England Review* and are anthologized in *Best New Poets 2013, The Breakbeat Poets: New American Poetry in the Age of Hip-Hop, Please Excuse This Poem: 100 New Poets for the Next Generation*, and elsewhere. Tarfia is the Nicholas Delbanco Visiting Professor of Poetry at the University of Michigan and co-directs Organic Weapon Arts with Jamaal May.

Katie Farris is the author of *boysgirls*, a collection of short-short fictions published in 2011 by Marick Press, as well as the co-translator of several books of poetry from the French, Chinese, and Russian. Her translations and original work have been published in many literary journals, including *Virginia Quarterly Review, Triquarterly, Hayden's Ferry, The Literary Review* and others. She is currently an Associate Professor at San Diego State University.

M.K. Foster's poetry won the 2013 *Gulf Coast* Poetry Prize, has been recognized with an Academy of American Poets Prize, and has appeared or is forthcoming in *Gulf Coast; Nashville Review; The Account; H.O.W. Journal; B O D Y; The Baltimore Review; Word Riot; The Journal; Ninth Letter; Radar Poetry*, and elsewhere. She holds an M.F.A. from the University of Maryland, College Park and currently pursues a Ph.D. in English Literature through the Hudson Strode Renaissance Program at the University of Alabama. "Because You Said *I Told You We Have Rock Rivers, But No Water*" is dedicated to and given for R.E.M., a star among lights.

Clifton Gachagua lives in Nairobi where he was born and raised. His poetry has appeared in *Kwani? '06* and *Saraba*. He recently finished work on a novel. He is also a scriptwriter and filmmaker.

Carmen Giménez Smith is the author of a memoir and four poetry collections—including *Milk and Filth*, finalist for the 2013 NBCC award in poetry. A CantoMundo Fellow, she teaches in the creative writing programs at New Mexico State University, while serving as the editor-in-chief of the literary journal *Puerto del Sol* and the publisher of Noemi Press.

Graça Graúna—Indigenous (Potiguara people/RN), writer, essayist. Graúna holds a Bachelor's, Master's and Doctoral degree in Letters from Universidade Federal de Pernambuco, and a Post-Doctorate in Literature, Education and Indigenous Rights at UMESP. She is an Assistant Professor at UPE, where she has coordinated the following projects: Literature and Human Rights, with MEC-SECAD; Training Course Project for Indigenous Teachers' Training at the State of Pernambuco; Project on the Heritage Potential of the Municipality of Garanhuns and its surroundings: literary production. She is leader of the Group for Comparative Studies: Literature and Interdisciplinarity (Grupec); Professor of the PROLETRAS Master course at UPE in the subjects of Children's and Juvenile Literature and Reading Literary Texts. She was Coordinator of the Children's and Juvenile Literature Thematic Commission at the III PROFLETRAS National Forum (May, 2014), and is editor of *Impressões de leitura do texto literário* (Published by Todas as Musas, São Paulo), a book of collaborations of 18 recent Master's graduates from Profletras, UPE. Graúna runs the blog: *Tecido de vozes – literatura e interculturalismo*: www.tecidodevozes.blogspot.com

francine j. harris is a 2015 NEA fellow whose first collection, *allegiance*, was a finalist for the 2013 Kate Tufts Discovery and PEN Open Book Award. Her second book, *Play Dead*, is forthcoming from Alice James Books. Her work has appeared in *Poetry, Boston Review, Rattle, Ninth Letter* and *Ploughshares*, among others. Originally from Detroit, she is a Cave Canem fellow and is currently a Writer in Residence at Washington University in St. Louis.

Bob Hicok was born in 1960 in Michigan and worked for many years in the automotive die industry. A published poet long before he earned his MFA, Hicok is the author of several collections of poems, including *The Legend of Light*, winner of the Felix Pollak Prize in Poetry in 1995 and named a 1997 ALA Booklist Notable Book of the Year; *Plus Shipping* (1998); *Animal Soul* (2001), a finalist for the National Book Critics Circle Award; *Insomnia Diary* (2004); *This Clumsy Living* (2007), which received the Rebekah Johnson Bobbitt National Prize for Poetry from the Library of Congress; *Words for Empty, Words for Full* (2010); and *Elegy Owed* (2013), a finalist for the National Book Critics Circle Award. His work has been selected numerous times for the Best American Poetry series. Hicok has won Pushcart Prizes and fellowships from the Guggenheim Foundation and the National Endowment for the Arts, and has taught creative writing at Western Michigan University and Virginia Tech.

Lizz Huerta is a Southern California based writer, poet, novelist in progress who paints wrought iron to pay the bills. She also works with literary arts non-profit So Say We All and is a VONA alum. Find her on Twitter: @lizzhuerta.

Ishion Hutchinson was born in Port Antonio, Jamaica and is the author of *Far District: Poems* (Peepal Tree Press).

Lauren Jensen-Deegan lives in Eugene, Oregon. Among other publications, her poetry has been included in *The Best American Poetry*, been featured as a Poet's Sampler in the *Boston Review* and selected as a finalist for the James Wright Poetry Award and Fineline

Competition in which both selections appeared in the *Mid-American Review*.

Amaud Jamaul Johnson is the author of two poetry collections, *Darktown Follies* (Tupelo 2013) and *Red Summer* (2006). A former Wallace Stegner Fellow in Poetry at Stanford University, and Cave Canem Fellow, his honors include a Pushcart Prize, the Hurston/Wright Legacy Award, the Edna Meudt Book Award, and the Dorset Prize. His work has appeared in *Best American Poetry, Southern Review, Crazyhorse, Narrative Magazine* and elsewhere. He teaches in the MFA Program in Creative Writing at the University of Wisconsin-Madison.

Claire Kageyama-Ramakrishnan's first book, *Shadow Mountain*, won the Four Way Books Intro Book Prize, and was published by Four Way Books; her second book, *Bear, Diamonds and Crane* was published by Four Way Books in 2011. In addition to publishing these books, she is a full-time English instructor at Houston Community College in Houston, Texas, a graduate of the Ph.D. in Literature and Creative Writing program at University of Houston, where she was a Cambor Fellow; a graduate of the M.A. literature program at University of California at Berkeley, and graduate of the M.F.A. in poetry program at University of Virginia, where she was a Henry Hoyns Fellow. She lives in Houston with her husband, daughter, and three cats.

Ilya Kaminsky is a poet, translator, and essayist who lives in San Diego.

Joan Naviyuk Kane is Inupiaq with family from King Island and Mary's Igloo, Alaska. She received a 2009 Whiting Writers' Award for her first poetry collection, *The Cormorant Hunter's Wife* (2009), and her second collection, *Hyperboreal* (2013), was chosen as the winner of the 2012 AWP Donald Hall Prize in Poetry and the 2014 American Book Award and is available from the University of Pittsburgh Press. She has received both an individual artist award (2007) and an artist fellowship (2013) from the Rasmuson Foundation, a fellowship from the Alaska State Council on the Arts (2009), the Alaska Conservation Foundation's Native Writers on the Environment award (2010), a Literature Fellowship from the Native Arts and Cultures Foundation (2012), a Creative Vision Award from United States Artists (2013) and an Alaska Literary Award (2014). She was the Indigenous Writer-in-Residence at the School for Advanced Research and artist/scholar-in-residence with the Polar Lab at the Anchorage Museum in 2014 and is faculty in the MFA Program in Creative Writing at the Institute for American Indian Arts. A graduate of Harvard College and Columbia University's School of the Arts, she lives in Anchorage, Alaska, with her husband and sons.

Katherine Larson's *Radial Symmetry* (Yale University Press, 2011) was selected by Louise Glück as the winner of the Yale Series of Younger Poets. Her poems have appeared in many journals, including *Poetry, The Kenyon Review, AGNI, Orion,* and *Poetry Northwest*. Her work has been honored by a Kate Tufts Discovery Award, a Ruth Lilly Fellowship, a Levis Reading Prize, and an Arizona Commission on the Arts Research and Development Grant. She currently lives in Northern Virginia with her family.

Mariama J. Lockington calls many places home but currently lives in Lansing, Michigan. She is published in *The Comstock Review* poetry journal (2009), *Sparkle and*

Blink Issue 3.8 (July 2012), *Uncommon Core: Contemporary poems for learning and living* (Red Beard Press, 2013) and is a San Francisco Literary Death Match champion (Episode 46).

Mariama performs her work around the country and teaches writing workshops for various youth organizations. She holds a Masters in Education from Lesley University and an MFA in Poetry from San Francisco State University. When she is not writing or teaching, you'll find Mariama singing karaoke, watching Buffy the Vampire Slayer, or re-reading her favorite book, *Sula* by Toni Morrison.

Tariq Luthun is a Palestinian-American writer & strategist from Detroit, MI. He is currently an MFA candidate for poetry at Warren Wilson College. Among other things, Luthun is the Social Media Director of Organic Weapon Arts, a board member of the nonprofit Write A House, and is the Director of the Ann Arbor Poetry Slam. His work has appeared in *The Offing* and *Button Poetry*.

He is a deep dish pizza evangelist best described as the end-result of Drake falsetto-rapping Edward Said's *Orientalism*.

Thomas Lux has two books forthcoming in 2016: a book of poetry, *To the Left of Time* (Houghton Mifflin Hourcourt), and an edited volume, *Selected Poems of Bill Knott* (Farrar, Straus and Giroux). He is the Bourne Chair in Poetry at the Georgia Institute of Technology.

Travis Macdonald was recently named a 2014 Pew Fellow in the Arts. He is the author of two full-length books – *The O Mission Repo [vol.1]* (Fact-Simile Editions) and *N7ostradamus* (BlazeVox Books) – as well as several chapbooks, including: *Basho's Phonebook* (E-ratio), *BAR/koans* (Erg Arts), *Sight & Sigh* (Beard of Bees), *Time* (Stoked Press) and *Hoop Cores* (Knives, Forks and Spoons Press). He is a copywriter by day and by night he co-edits Fact-Simile Editions (www.fact-simile.com) with his wife JenMarie.

Carolann Caviglia Madden is a poet, translator, and Navy brat whose work has appeared or is forthcoming in *Cactus Heart, Women in Clothes, Souvenir, Witch Craft Magazine, Yalobusha Review, World Literature Today*, and elsewhere. She is a founding editor of Locked Horn Press, an Assistant Poetry Editor at *Gulf Coast*, a member of Scholars Without Borders, and is a PhD candidate at the University of Houston.

David Maduli is a writer, veteran public school teacher, active deejay and father. Born in San Francisco, he is a longtime resident of Oakland and winner of the 2011 Joy Harjo Poetry Prize.

Nick Makoha represented Uganda at Poetry Parnassus as part of the Cultural Olympiad held in London. A former Writer in Residence for Newham Libraries, his 1-man-Show My Father & Other Superheroes debuted to sold-out performances at 2013 London Literature Festival and is currently on tour. He has been a panelist at both the inaugural Being a Man Festival (Fatherhood: Past, Present & Future) and Women of the World Festival (Bringing Up Boys). In 2005 award-winning publisher Flippedeye launched its pamphlet series with his debut *The Lost Collection of an Invisible Man*. Part of his soon-to-be-published first full collection, *The Second Republic,* is in the anthology *Seven New Generation African Poets* (Slapering Hol Press). Nick recently won the Brunel African Poetry prize and has poems that appear in the *The Poetry Review, Rialto, The Triquarterly Review* and the *Boston Review.*

Sally Wen Mao is the author of *Mad Honey Symposium* (Alice James Books, 2014). She is the current Singapore Creative Writing Residency 2015 Resident.

Adrian Matejka is the author of *The Devil's Garden* (Alice James Books, 2003) and *Mixology* (Penguin, 2009), which was a winner of the 2008 National Poetry Series. His most recent book, *The Big Smoke*, was awarded the Anisfield-Wolf Book Award and was a finalist for the 2013 National Book Award and 2014 Pulitzer Prize.

Erika Meitner is the author of four books of poems, including *Copia* (BOA Editions, 2014), *Makeshift Instructions for Vigilant Girls* (Anhinga Press, 2011), and *Ideal Cities* (HarperCollins, 2010), which was a 2009 National Poetry Series winner. In 2015, she was the US-UK Fulbright Distinguished Scholar in Creative Writing at the Seamus Heaney Centre for Poetry at Queen's University Belfast. She is currently an Associate Professor of English at Virginia Tech, where she also directs the MFA program in Creative Writing.

Jennifer Minniti-Shippey is the Managing Editor of *Poetry International* literary journal, and a professor at San Diego State University. Her chapbook, *Done Dating DJs*, won the 2009 Fool For Poetry Chapbook competition, presented by the Munster Literature Centre of Cork, Ireland. Her most recent chapbook, *Earth's Horses & Boys*, was published by Finishing Line Press in March, 2013. Her work has appeared in *Tar River Poetry, Jackson Hole Review, In Posse Review, San Diego Poetry Annual*, and the *San Diego Union-Tribune*, among others.

Michael Mlekoday is the author of *The Dead Eat Everything* (Kent State University Press, 2014), a National Poetry Slam Champion, and a doctoral student at the University of California, Davis. Mlekoday's poems have appeared in *Verse Daily, The BreakBeat Poets, cream city review, Salt Hill*, and other venues.

Felix Mnthali was born and grew up in Malawi in south central Africa. He was educated at Malawi University and Cambridge University in England. He returned to Africa, and as a visitor at the University of Ibadan in Nigeria, he wrote and privately published *Echoes from Ibadan* (1961). Back in his homeland he became the head of the department of English at Malawi University. His published works include a book of poetry, *When Sunset Comes to Sapitwa* (1980), and a novel, *My Dear Anniversary* (1992). He was also included in the 1984 anthology *The Penguin Book of Modern African Poetry*.

Carrie Moniz's poetry and reviews have appeared in *Ploughshares, Superstition Review, Yellow Medicine Review, Suisun Valley Review, Third Wednesday, Corium Magazine, An Island of Egrets* & *scent of rain haiku* anthologies, *A Year In Ink Vol. 4 & 5,* Web del Sol Review of Books, and elsewhere. She is a founding editor of *The California Journal of*

Poetics. She divides her time between the San Francisco Bay Area and San Diego.

David Mura is a poet, creative nonfiction writer, critic, playwright and performance artist. A Sansei or third generation Japanese American, Mura has written two memoirs: *Turning Japanese: Memoirs of a Sansei* (Anchor-Random), which won a 1991 Josephine Miles Book Award from the Oakland PEN and was listed in the New York Times Notable Books of Year, and *Where the Body Meets Memory: An Odyssey of Race, Sexuality and Identity* (1996, Anchor).

Mura's second book of poetry, *The Colors of Desire* (1995, Anchor), won the Carl Sandburg Literary Award from the Friends of the Chicago Public Library. His first, *After We Lost Our Way* (Carnegie Mellon U. Press), won the 1989 National Poetry Series Contest. He has also written the chapbook, *A Male Grief: Notes on Pornography & Addiction* (Milkweed Editions). His book of critical essays, *Song for Uncle Tom, Tonto & Mr. Moto: Poetry & Identity*, was published by the U. of Michigan Press in its Poets on Poetry series in 2002. His third book of poetry, *Angels for the Burning*, was published by Boa Editions Ltd. in 2004.

Mura has received a Lila Wallace-Reader's Digest Writers' Award, a US/Japan Creative Artist Fellowship, two NEA Literature Fellowships, two Bush Foundation Fellowships, four Loft-McKnight Awards, several Minnesota State Arts Board grants, and a Discovery/ The Nation Award. He teaches at Hamline University, VONA (Voices of the Nation Association), and the Stonecoast MFA program. Mura lives in Minneapolis with his wife, Dr. Susan Sencer, and three children.

Angel Nafis is an Ann Arbor, Michigan native and Cave Canem Fellow. Her work has appeared in *POETRY, The Rumpus, FOUND Magazine's Requiem for a Paper Bag, Decibels, The Rattling Wall, Union Station Magazine, The Bear River Review, MUZZLE Magazine, Mosaic Magazine* and more. In 2011 she represented the LouderArts poetry project at both the Women of the World Poetry Slam and the National Poetry Slam. She is an Urban Word NYC Mentor and the founder, curator, and host of the Greenlight Bookstore Poetry Salon. Facilitating acclaimed generative writing workshops and reading poems in universities, high schools, bookstores, detention centers, theaters, teen centers, bars, conferences, and tattoo parlors across the United States and Canada. With poet Morgan Parker she is The Other BlackGirl Collective. Author of *BlackGirl Mansion* (Red Beard Press/ New School Poetics, 2012) she lives in Brooklyn with artist/musician/writer Shira Erlichman and an orange cat named Deuces.

Binh H. Nguyen studied literature and creative writing with Jim Crenner at Hobart College, where he founded and edited *SCRY! A Nexus of Politics and the Arts* (Anne Carson was among the contributors). He was a semi-finalist in the 2015 Joy Harjo Poetry Contest. Binh conducted an interview with the American novelist-poet Katherine Towler and co-translated the poems of Mario Bojórquez for *Poetry International*. He writes theater reviews for the *San Diego Reader*. Binh is currently working on his MFA degree in poetry writing at SDSU and is the founder and curator of *Thru a Soft Tube*, a monthly reading series in San Diego.

A native of California, **Diana Khoi Nguyen**'s poems appear in P*oetry, Denver Quarterly, Gulf Coast, Kenyon Review Online*, and *PEN America*, among others. She has also received the Fred and Edith B. Herman Award from the Academy of American Poets and Scotti Merrill Award from the Key West Literary Seminars, as well as four Bread Loaf Writers Conference scholarships, an Archie D. and Bertha H. Walker Scholarship from the Provincetown Fine Arts Work Center, and the Lucille Clifton Scholarship from the Community of Writers at Squaw Valley. A Ruth Lilly Fellowship finalist and Bread Loaf Bakeless Camargo fellow, she earned her MFA from Columbia University and was recently the Roth Resident in poetry at Bucknell University. Currently, she is a PhD candidate in creative writing at the University of Denver. www.dianakhoinguyen.com

Nicole Parizeau is former senior editor at *Whole Earth* Magazine and principal editor at University of California, Berkeley's Lawrence Hall of Science. She is a winner of the Bill Holm Witness Poetry Award and has written or contributed to several books on science and education. Nicole's poetry and prose appear in *Folio, Poecology, Emrys Journal, Written River*, and *The Fourth River*. www.nicoleparizeau.net

Jonathan Rodley studies poetry and teaches composition at San Diego State University.

Patrick Rosal is the author of four books of poetry, most recently, *Brooklyn Antediluvian*. His essays and poetry have appeared in *The New York Times, Tin House, American Poetry Review, Harvard Review, Grantland*, and many other journals and magazines. His writing has been collected in *Best American Poetry*, the *Norton Anthology Language for a New Century, Dandániw ti Ilokano: mga tulang Ilokano, 1621-2014*, a comprehensive collection of poems written in the Philippine language of Ilokano. His work has been translated into Spanish, Tagalog, and Greek. And he has published or performed in South Africa, the Philippines, many venues and festivals in Europe, the Caribbean, Latin America as well as throughout the United States. Highlights of his performances and collaborations include features at Lincoln Center, the Whitney Museum, Mar de Plata Film Festival, and many other events and venues. He is a former Fulbright fellow and currently a full-time faculty member of the MFA program at Rutgers University-Camden.

Craig Santos Perez is a native Chamoru from the Pacific Island of Guåhan/Guam. He is the co-founder of Ala Press, co-star of the poetry album *Undercurrent*, and author of three collections of poetry: *from unincorporated territory [hacha], from unincorporated territory [saina]*, and *from unincorporated territory [guma']*. He is an Associate Professor in the English Department and affiliate faculty with the Center for Pacific Islands Studies and the Indigenous Politics Program at the University of Hawai'i, Manoa.

Staci R. Schoenfeld—A recipient of a 2015 NEA Fellowship for poetry, grants from the Barbara Deming Memorial Fund and the Kentucky Foundation for Women, Staci R. Schoenfeld's poems appear in or are forthcoming from *Washington Square, Mid-American Review, North Dakota Quarterly, Muzzle, and Southern Humanities Review*, among others. She is a first-year PhD student at the University of South Dakota, assistant editor for poetry at South Dakota Review, and an assistant editor at Sundress Publications.

Matthew Shenoda is a writer and professor whose poems and essays have appeared in a variety of newspapers, journals, radio programs and anthologies. He has been twice nominated for a Pushcart Prize and his work has been supported by the California Arts Council and the Lannan Foundation, among others.

His debut collection of poems, *Somewhere Else* (Coffee House Press), was named one of 2005's debut books of the year by *Poets & Writers* Magazine and was winner of a 2006 American Book Award. He is also the author of *Seasons of Lotus, Seasons of Bone* (BOA Editions Ltd.), editor of *Duppy Conqueror: New & Selected Poems by Kwame Dawes*, and most recently author of *Tahrir Suite: Poems* (TriQuarterly Books/Northwestern University Press) winner of the 2015 Arab American Book Award. *Bearden's Odyssey: An Anthology of Poets Responding to the Art of Romare Bearden*, edited by Shenoda and Kwame Dawes will be released by Northwestern University Press in 2016.

Shenoda lectures widely and has taught extensively in the fields of ethnic studies and creative writing. He has held several faculty and administrative positions at various institutions and is currently Associate Professor in the Department of Creative Writing at Columbia College Chicago. Additionally, Shenoda has served on the Board of Directors of several arts and education organizations and is a founding editor of the African Poetry Book Series. He lives with his family in Evanston, Illinois.

David Shook is a poet and translator in Los Angeles, where he runs Phoneme Media. His book *Our Obsidian Tongues* was longlisted for the International Dylan Thomas Prize in 2013. His many translations include books by Mario Bellatin, Tedi López Mills, and Víctor Terán. In addition to his writing, Shook has produced literary films in places like Bangladesh, Cuba, and Equatorial Guinea. He recently edited *Like a New Sun: New Indigenous Mexican Poetry*, featuring poetry from six different indigenous Mexican languages.

Javier Sicilia is a Mexican poet, journalist, essayist and social critic. Sicilia's last poem, written for his son, who was murdered by cartel thugs and torturers, declares: "this is my last poem,/I no longer have poetry in my heart." Despite his disavowal of writing poetry, Sicilia still considers himself a poet, now performing that office's prophetic role, sharing in the public storytelling required for community healing, in open defiance of the culture of fear propagated by cartels and the Mexican government alike. Sicilia had established himself as an important Mexican poet and writer over the past thirty years, winning the Ariel Award for his work in film, the José Fuentes Mares Award for his novel *The Baptist*, and the 2009 Aguascalientes Prize for his last book of poetry, *Desert Triptych*.

Richard Siken is a poet, painter, filmmaker, and an editor at Spork Press. He is a recipient of two Arizona Commission on the Arts grants, two Lannan Residency Fellowships, and a Literature Fellowship in Poetry from the National Endowment for the Arts.

Jane Springer is author of two collections of poetry, *Dear Blackbird*, and *Murder Ballad*. Her honors include a Pushcart, an NEA fellowship, a Best American Poetry prize, and a

Whiting Writers' Award. She lives in upstate, New York, with her husband, their son, and their two dogs, Leisure-Lee and Azy.

A 2015 Pew Fellow in the Arts, **Brian Teare** is the recipient of poetry fellowships from the National Endowment for the Arts, the MacDowell Colony, the Headlands Center for the Arts, the Fund for Poetry, and the American Antiquarian Society. He is the author of four critically acclaimed books—*The Room Where I Was Born*, *Sight Map*, the Lambda Award-winning *Pleasure*, and *Companion Grasses*, a finalist for the Kingsley Tufts Award. His fifth book is *The Empty Form Goes All the Way to Heaven* (Ahsahta, 2015). An Assistant Professor at Temple University, he lives in South Philadelphia, where he makes books by hand for his micropress, Albion Books.

Truth Thomas is a singer-songwriter and poet born in Knoxville, Tennessee and raised in Washington, DC. He is the founder of Cherry Castle Publishing and studied creative writing at Howard University under Dr. Tony Medina. Thomas earned his MFA in poetry at New England College. His collections include: *Party of Black*, *A Day of Presence*, *Bottle of Life*, *My TV is Not the Boss of Me* (a children's book, illustrated by Cory Thomas) and *Speak Water*, winner of the 2013 NAACP Image Award for Outstanding Literary Work in Poetry. He serves on the editorial board of Tidal Basin Review and is a former writer-in-residence for the Howard County Poetry and Literature Society (HoCoPoLitSo). His poems have appeared in over 100 publications, including *The 100 Best African American Poems* (edited by Nikki Giovanni).

Brian Turner's latest book, *My Life as a Foreign Country: A Memoir* is published by W.W. Norton & Company in the US and Canada, and by Jonathan Cape/Random House in the UK and Ireland. His two collections of poetry: *Here, Bullet* (Alice James Books, 2005; Bloodaxe Books, 2007) and *Phantom Noise* (Alice James Books, 2010; Bloodaxe Books in October of 2010) have also been published in Swedish by Oppenheim forlag. His poems have been published and translated in Arabic, Chinese, Dutch, French, German, Hebrew, Italian, Polish, Serbo-Croatian, Spanish, and Swedish.

His poetry and essays have been published in *The New York Times*, *National Geographic*, *Poetry Daily*, *The Georgia Review*, *Virginia Quarterly Review* and other journals.

Turner was featured in the documentary film Operation Homecoming: Writing the Wartime Experience, which was nominated for an Academy Award. He received a USA Hillcrest Fellowship in Literature, an NEA Literature Fellowship in Poetry, the Amy Lowell Traveling Fellowship, a US-Japan Friendship Commission Fellowship, the Poets' Prize, and a Fellowship from the Lannan Foundation. His most recent book of poetry, *Phantom Noise*, was short-listed for the T.S. Eliot Prize in England. His work has appeared on National Public Radio, the BBC, Newshour with Jim Lehrer, Here and Now, and on Weekend America, among others.

Turner earned an MFA from the University of Oregon before serving for seven years in the US Army. He directs the MFA program at Sierra Nevada College and serves as a contributing editor at The Normal School. Brian is married to Ilyse Kusnetz (poet and author of *Small Hours* from Truman State University Press). They live in Orlando, Florida.

Sarah Vap is the author of five collections of poetry, the most recent are *Arco Iris* (Saturnalia Books, 2012) and *End of a Sentimental Journey* (Noemi Press, 2013). She is a recipient of a National Endowment of the Arts Grant for Literature, and her book *Viability* (Penguin, 2015) was selected for the National Poetry Series by Mary Jo Bang.

Annie Won is a poet, yoga teacher, and medicinal chemist who resides in Medford, MA. She is a Kundiman Fellow and a Juniper Writing Institute scholarship recipient. Her chapbook with Brenda Iijima, *Once Upon a Building Block*, published with Horse Less Press (2014) and individual chapbooks, *so i can sleep* (Nous-Zot Press, 2015) and *did the wind blow it* (Dusie Kollektiv, 2015) are also available. Her work has appeared in venues such as *New Delta Review, Entropy, Delirious Hem, TheThePoetry, TENDE RLION*, and others. Her critical reviews can be seen at *American Microreviews and Interviews*.

Monika Zobel's writing has appeared in *The Cincinnati Review, Redivider, DIAGRAM, Beloit Poetry Journal, Mid-American Review, Guernica Magazine, West Branch, Best New Poets 2010*, and elsewhere. Her book, *An Instrument for Leaving*, was selected by Dorothea Lasky for the 2013 Slope Editions Book Prize. A Senior Editor at *The California Journal of Poetics* and Fulbright alumna, Zobel currently lives in Bremen, Germany.

CREDITS

Abinader, Elmaz. "Heartwood" appears in *This House, My Bones*, Aquarius Press/Willow Books, 2014. © 2014 by Elmaz Abinader. All rights reserved. http://willowlit.net/

Awoonor, Kofi. Reproduced from *The Promise of Hope: New and Selected Poems, 1964-2013* by Kofi Awoonor by permission of the University of Nebraska Press. © 2014 by the Board of Regents of the University of Nebraska.

Bojórquez, Mario. "A orillas del río Delaware frente a Camden y mirando las luces del Walt Whitman Bridge," and "Museo Guggenheim" appear in *Pretzels*, Colección Gláphyras, 2005. © 2005 by Mario Bojórquez. All rights reserved. "At the banks of the Delaware River Waterfront facing Camden and watching the lights of the Walt Whitman Bridge" and "Guggenheim Museum" were translated from the Spanish by Hari Alluri, Binh H. Nguyen, and Jonathan Rodley. Copyright © 2016 by Hari Alluri, Binh H. Nguyen, and Jonathan Rodley.

Borzutzky, Daniel. "Dream Song #16" *In the Murmurs of the Rotten Carcass Economy*: Nightboat Books, 2015. © 2015 by Daniel Borzutzky. All rights reserved. http://www.nightboat.org.

Brown, Derrick Westin: "Halle Tells How They Broke Him" originally appears in Derrick Westin Brown's *Wisdom Teeth* (PM Press/Busboys and Poets Press, www.pmpress.org).

Calderón, Alí. "Constantinopla" appears in *Las correspondencias* (Visor, 2015). Copyright © 2015 by Alí Calderón. "[Kentucky]" appears in *Imago Prima*, (Universidad Autónoma de Zacatecas, 2005). Copyright © 2005 by Alí Calderón. All rights reserved. "Constantinopla" and "[Kentucky]" were translated from the Spanish by Ana Bosch and Karla Cordero. Copyright © 2016 by Ana Bosch and Karla Cordero.

Chambers, Grady. "Dispatch: Bamyan, Helmand, Baghlan, Ghor, 2008" first appeared in *Devil's Lake*: Spring, 2013. © 2013 by Grady Chambers.

Chang, Jennifer. "This Corner of the Western World," *The History of Anatomy*. University of Georgia Press, 2008. Copyright © 2008 by Jennifer Chang. Reprinted by permission of The University of Georgia Press.

Cob, Briceida Cuevas. "U áak' abil tuchibil uj," and "In k'aaba'" appear in *Ti' u billil in nook': Del dobladillo de mi ropa*: Literatura Indígena Contemporánea, 2008. Copyright © 2008 by Briceida Cuevas Cob. All rights reserved. Reprinted with permission of the author. "Night of the Eclipse," and "My Name" were translated from Maya via the author's Spanish language translation by Carolann Caviglia Madden. Copyright © 2016 by Carolann Caviglia Madden.

Cordero, Karla. "This Skin Be," first appeared in *Drunk in a Midnight Choir*: June 2, 2015. Copyright © 2015 by Karla Cordero.

Cruz, Cynthia. "Sparks, Nevada" and "Twelve in Yellow-Weed at the Edge" from *Ruin*. Copyright © 2016 by Cynthia Cruz. Reprinted with the permission of The Permissions Company, Inc., on behalf of the author and Alice James Books, www.alicejamesbooks.org.

Day, Meg. "*Teenage Lesbian Couple Found In Texas Park With Gunshot Wounds to the Head*," *Last Psalm at Sea Level* (Barrow Street, 2014). All rights reserved.

Diaz, Natalie. "Other Small Thundering," and "Woman with No Legs." *When My Brother Was an Aztec*. Copper Canyon Press, 2012. Copyright © 2012 by Natalie Diaz. All rights reserved.

Dungy, Camille. "'Tis of thee, sweet land (a poem of found text,)" and "There are Seven Things I Know, and None of Them Is You," *Suck on the Marrow*. Red Hen Press, 2010. Copyright © 2010 by Camille Dungy. Reprinted with permission of the author.

Faizullah, Tarfia. "100 Bells" appears in *Poetry*: January, 2015. http://www.poetryfoundation.org Copyright © 2015 by Tarfia Faizullah.

Farris, Katie. "What We See in the Dark," appears in *Talisman*, Issue 42, 2014. © 2014 by Katie Farris www.talismanmag.net.

Gimenez Smith, Carmen. "Radicalization," from *Milk and Filth*, by Carmen Giménez Smith. © 2013 Carmen Giménez Smith. Reprinted by permission of the University of Arizona Press.

Graúna, Graça. "Caos climático" appears on *Overmundo*, October 2009, and "Manifesto—I" on *Overmundo*, February, 2010; they can also be found in *Collar de historias y lunas: Antología de poesía de mujeres indígenas de América Latina*, ed. Jennie Carrasco Molina: Ministerio Coordinador de Patrimonio, 2011. Copyright © 2009 & 2010 by Graça Graúna. Reprinted with permission of the author. "Climate Chaos," and "Manifesto 1" were translated from Portuguese via the author's Spanish language translation by Carolann Caviglia Madden. Copyright © 2016 by Carolann Caviglia Madden.

harris, francine j. "sift" reprinted from *allegiance* by francine j. harris. Copyright © 2012 Wayne State University Press. Reprinted with permission of the author.

Hicok, Bob. "Speaking American" from *Elegy Owed*. Copyright © 2014 by Bob Hicok. Reprinted with the permission of The Permissions Company, Inc., on behalf of Copper Canyon Press, www.coppercanyonpress.org.

Huerta, Lizz. "milking" appears in *West Trestle Review*, 2014. http://www.westtrestlereview.com. Copyright © 2014 by Lizz Huerta.

Hutchinson, Ishion. "A Surveryor's Journal" appears in *The Caribbean Review of Books*: February, 2009. Copyright © 2009 Ishion Hutchinson.

Jensen-Deegan, Lauren. "Only You, My Husband, as Smokey the Bear" first appeared in *Linebreak*: September, 2014. https://linebreak.org. Copyright © 2014 by Lauren Jensen-Deegan.

Johnson, Amaud Jamaul. "Pigmeat" from *Darktown Follies*. Published by Tupelo Press, Copyright 2013 by Amaud Jamaul Johnson. Used with permission.

Kageyama-Ramakrishnan, Claire. "Terzanelle: Manzanar Riot," from *Shadow Mountain*: Four Way Books, 2006. Copyright © 2006 by Claire Kageyama-Ramakrishnan. Reprinted with permission of Four Way Books. All rights reserved.

Kaminsky, Ilya. "We Lived Happily During the War" appears in *Poetry International*, 2013. © 2013 by Ilya Kaminsky www.poetryinternationalweb.net

Larson, Katherine. "Love at Thirty-two Degrees," from *Radial Symmetry*: Yale University Press, 2011. Copyright © 2011 by Katherine Larson. Reprinted with permission of Yale University Press. All rights reserved.

Luthun, Tariq. "New Rule" appears in *The Offing*, May 2015. Copyright © 2015 Tariq Luthun. www.theoffingmag.com

Lux, Thomas. "Lumps of Sugar on an Anthill," from *God Particles*. Houghton Mifflin Co., 2008. Copyright © 2008 by Thomas Lux. Reprinted with permission of the author.

Makoha, Nick. "Prayers for Exiled Poets," appears in *The Second Republic*, Slapering Hol Press, 2014. Copyright © 2014 by Nick Makoha.

Mao, Sally Wen. "Provenance: A Vivisection" appears in *Harvard Review Online*: April, 2015. Copyright © 2015 by Sally Wen Mao.

Meitner, Erika. "By Other Means" is from *Copia*: BOA Editions, 2014. Copyright © 2014 BOA Editions. All rights reserved.

Mnthali, Felix. "Neocolonialism" from *When Sunset Comes to Sapitwa*: Prentice Hall Press, 1983. Copyright © by Felix Mnthali, 1983.

Moniz, Carrie. "Year Two of Your Seven-Year Sentence: Midnight Ride to Yuma" appears in *Superstition Review*: Issue 9, Spring 2012. Copyright © 2012 by Carrie Moniz.

Mura, David, "Summers with the JACL." *In The Last Incantations: Poems*. Evanston: TriQuarterly Books/Northwestern University Press, 2014. Copyright © 2014 by David Mura. Published 2014 by TriQuarterly Books/ Northwestern University Press. All rights reserved.

Nafis, Angel. "Gravity" appears in Poetry: April, 2015, and also in *The BreakBeat Poets Anthology* (Haymarket Books, 2015). Copyright © 2015 by Angel Nafis.

Rosal, Patrick. "Delenda Undone," from *Bonesheperds*. Persea, 2011. Copyright © 2011 by Patrick Rosal. All rights reserved.

Schoenfeld, Staci R. "The Deconstruction of Dorothy Parker" appears in *Quaint*, Issue #3: Summer, 2014. © 2014 Staci Schoenfeld. http://quaintmagazine.com/

Sicilia, Javier. "Lo abierto" copyright © Javier Sicilia and Ediciones Era, 2011. Translated from the Spanish by David Shook. Copyright © David Shook, 2012.

Siken, Richard. "Landscape with a Blur of Conquerors" and "Detail of the Fire" from *War of the Foxes*. Copyright © 2015 by Richard Siken. Reprinted with the permission of The Permissions Company, Inc., on behalf of Copper Canyon Press, www.coppercanyonpress.org.

Springer, Jane. "Salt Hill," from *Murder Ballad*. Copyright © 2012 by Jane Springer. Reprinted with the permission of The Permissions Company, Inc., on behalf of Alice James Books, www.alicejamesbooks.org.

Thomas, Truth. "Urban Warming" first appeared in *Poetry*: January, 2016. http://

www.poetryfoundation.org. Copyright © 2016 by Truth Thomas.

Turner, Brian. "Sadiq" from *Here, Bullet*. Copyright © 2005 by Brian Turner. "Phantom Noise" from *Phantom Noise*. Copyright © 2010 by Brian Turner. Both reprinted with the permission of The Permissions Company, Inc., on behalf of Alice James Books, www.alicejamesbooks.org.

Vap, Sarah. "bluebells. blueballs. ballerinas." appears in *La Petite Zine*. Issue 20: Spring, 2007. © 2007 by Sarah Vap. http://www.lapetitezine.org/

Zobel, Monika. "The Immigrant Searches the Map for Countries Larger Than His Palm" appears in *An Instrument for Leaving*, published by Slope Editions, 2014. © by Monika Zobel. All rights reserved. Reprinted with permission of Slope Editions. http://www.slopeeditions.org

These pages include information on poems that have been published both online, and in print, prior to appearing in Read America(s). Locked Horn Press has made every effort to contact rights holders, and to credit previous publications correctly. We apologize for any publications that may have been overlooked, or credited incorrectly. Please do contact us with any questions.